T0277395

# Praise for
# *Dare to Author!*

"Lior Arussy has done it again. *Dare to Author!* is a transformative resource for activating the power of personal narrative. This book will help you examine your internal stories and understand how those stories shape your decisions. More important, it will provide the tools needed to author your success-and-significance story. This book is a must-read for anyone seeking an effective path of self-discovery and profound impact."

**—Joseph Michelli, Ph.D.**, *New York Times* #1 best-selling author of *Stronger Through Adversity*, *The Starbucks Experience*, *The Airbnb Way*, and *Driven to Delight*

"Once again, Lior shares his insights on excellence and living a meaningful and purpose-filled life. *Dare to Author!* interweaves leadership lessons, insights from social and behavioral sciences, theology, personal vulnerability and business acumen to offer a guide to leading through intentionality. It is a must-read for anyone looking to thrive in their personal and professional journey."

**—Harry Hynekamp,** Vice President Guest Experiences, AMB Sports and Entertainment

"The story that people understand about you, your company, and your life is based on how you do what you do. How do you honor people's lives? How do you guide your people to have the courage and permission to do that? How do you evolve as your business and customers' needs evolve to continue to improve lives? Lior's book is a savvy guidebook for how to achieve this elusive approach that few can achieve! A great read—and worth your time!"

—**Jeanne Bliss,** Author, Chief Customer Officer 2.0, Co-founder, Customer Experience Professionals Association (CXPA)

"Lior once again provides a manual for success and confidence with candor and bares his innermost feelings. I particularly liked Lior's anecdote about the institution that was seeing a downward trend in donations as alumni evolved but hadn't changed how they talked to these students or alums. When realized, businesses almost always see an uptick, so it is a great callout. I also think the story about the local youth group director bringing his group to New Orleans was great and can help anyone realize one small step can be the first to greater work."

—**Alison Brod,** CEO Alison Brod Marketing + Communication

# DARE
# TO
*Author!*

# DARE
# TO
*Author!*

## TAKE CHARGE OF THE
## NARRATIVE OF YOUR LIFE

# LIOR ARUSSY

GREENLEAF
BOOK GROUP PRESS

Published by Greenleaf Book Group Press
Austin, Texas
www.gbgpress.com

Distributed by Greenleaf Book Group

For ordering information or special discounts for bulk purchases, please contact Greenleaf Book Group at PO Box 91869, Austin, TX 78709, 512.891.6100.

Design and composition by Greenleaf Book Group
Cover design by Greenleaf Book Group and Lauren Smith
Cover image: ©iStockphoto.com/t_kimura

Publisher's Cataloging-in-Publication data is available.

Print ISBN: 979-8-88645-250-1

eBook ISBN: 979-8-88645-251-8

To offset the number of trees consumed in the printing of our books, Greenleaf donates a portion of the proceeds from each printing to the Arbor Day Foundation. Greenleaf Book Group has replaced over 50,000 trees since 2007.

Printed in the United States of America on acid-free paper

24 25 26 27 28 29 30 31    10 9 8 7 6 5 4 3 2 1

First Edition

*"I am breaking," said the light and transformed into a rainbow.*

—Nerya Yakov, Nahal Oz

*Dedicated to all the lights that transformed their breaking points into beautiful, inspiring rainbows. And to all of you who will in the future.*

# Contents

# First Words

"Lior, why don't you speak to us about your next book?"

I paused. I was on a call briefing a CEO about a presentation I was going to give to the executive team regarding innovation management. I wasn't stunned by the question because it was off topic. I was stunned because there was no book.

I stammered, "Well, I'm not exactly sure what you mean because I don't have a next book."

"Sure you do," the CEO insisted. "Just speak about that when you do your presentation."

And with that, he hung up.

My mind went blank. What could he mean? I had some nascent ideas that I had published in an article, but the distance was vast between an article and a new book. But for this CEO, "no" was not in his vocabulary. So I had thirty days to somehow craft brand-new content and share it with the executive team. From that, this book was born.

I never intended to write this book. But after delivering the presentation and based on the positive feedback, I started to work on it. It was a journey that took me to three continents and required admitting a multitude of personal experiences and insights. Thanks to my client Ben Salzman, the CEO of Sheboygan-based insurance company Acuity, here we are. This book all started because of him, so let's give credit where credit is due.

When he issued the challenge, I began by looking at my work in the last two decades of helping employees and organizations deal with change and transformation. What caused them to succeed or fail?

In turning this concept over in my mind, I discovered one critical factor that determined failure or success: Failure always followed when employees viewed themselves as victims of change. When they felt in control of the narrative, they led change with pride. The story they crafted around the change was core to their ability to mobilize change and transformation. This discovery and experience gave me the foundation to write this book.

Ben was right. I had another book in me. But beyond the professional aspect of my life that drove me to ultimately write the book, this quest was personal. Working on this book helped me author my own life story. When I say authoring your story, I mean taking the facts that were sometimes not according to your plan and transforming them into a purposeful chapter of your life full of insights that you're excited to tell others, that build your strength and resilience. As I was writing this book, I had to face losses, failures, betrayals of friends, and many other recent and past experiences, good and bad, that I had not fully authored yet in my story. I had to confront my own biases, convictions, paradigms, obstacles, fears, and unexpected life events that threw me off and made me feel like a floating, helpless leaf carried into unexpected destinations. I needed to gain control over that amalgamation of confusing, depressing emotions. I didn't want to be a helpless victim in my own life. I wanted to take back control of the narrative and how I felt about it.

COVID-19 definitely contributed to the state of helplessness I found myself in. That year I was supposed to visit Chile, Mexico, Amsterdam, Vancouver, Alaska, Shanghai, New York, London, and Madrid. Instead, I spent 2020 chasing airlines to get refunds. It was a total personal disaster, one that plunged me into a victim mentality. Writing this book helped me to make sense of the unexpected, transforming from plunging into victimhood and instead emerging as a victor. Taking back control of the narrative, even and especially of the unexpected events, took those chapters I used to shrink from into stories I am proud to tell.

There is an old story about a shoemaker in the US who wanted to expand his business internationally. He sent two people to Africa to examine the opportunity. The first person called him back saying everyone in Africa is walking barefoot and therefore there is no need for shoes here. The second person called and said that no one in Africa has shoes and therefore the market is ripe for a shoe company to come in and take advantage of this great opportunity. The facts were the same, but the stories were different. Both people viewed the same factual condition, yet they shared a completely different story with their boss.

As we discuss in the book, it is not the facts that matter but rather the stories we develop around them. That is why intentional authoring is so critical.

Authoring is the process of converting life experiences into future strength, resilience, and elevated performance. My goal in sharing these insights, findings, experiences, and ideas with you is simple: to provide you with a perspective and tool kit that may help you do exactly the same and become the protagonist of your life story, one you will be proud of no matter what happens.

By authoring the story of your life, you make a choice to become a victor even in the face of helplessness. You develop your journey to a life story you get to write while training the muscle of resilience. Authoring your life story is taking charge of every aspect of it, no matter what the original plan was or the factors in it that were out of your control.

Authoring your life challenges is the one power you have control over, no matter what. Authoring is not restricted to professional authors. We are all telling stories and authoring in one way or another. We all live in stories that comfort us through our life or encourage us to act courageously. Stories are what we craft to make life make sense and livable. How you tell a story isn't up to your circumstances. It is up to *you*, the author.

In this book, I challenge you to be intentional about the authoring process and to take charge of the stories you create for yourself and the people around you. You may experience this book in its totality and view it as a journey to live a better, more purposeful life. Alternatively, you can focus on relevant chapters in specific moments, such as the chapter about impostor syndrome or leading with storytelling.

As more and more people feel lonely and depression becomes prevalent, I hope that engaging with the process of authoring your life story will assist in shifting you from a state of victimhood to a state of hopefulness. I know the power of authoring in my work with my clients. By shifting the story, we point people to the power they do have and away from the power they don't have. Every person, no matter what their position is, has some sort of power. When we experience victimhood, we focus on the power we don't have. When we author our life story, we develop the focus on the power we do have. The purpose of this book is to help you focus on those special powers you possess, and much more, that the world can benefit from.

The book is divided into three parts: *Author Why?*, *Author How?*, and *Author Now!* In the first part, we explore the case for authoring your life's story. We discuss the different listening lenses that cloud our facts and shape different stories in our life. We make the case that authoring our life story should be an intentional endeavor that can elevate our life from that of a victim to a victor.

In the second part, *Author How?*, we explore authoring from a storytelling process—managing the cynical voices in your head and the choice of words in our lives and examining how they shape our stories. This section develops a blueprint, guided by questions to enable you to start writing life chapters. The third part, *Author Now!*, invites you to start becoming the author and to apply the lessons. It explores the challenges and provides guidance on how to develop a life story over time. It also includes relevant chapters on applying stories in the workplace and discusses leadership through storytelling and how to launch successful projects. You'll see some prompts at the ends of chapters to help you begin authoring your story. Feel free to write directly in this book and return to your words as you are ready.

Life is about choices, even when you don't think you have them. One choice you do have is whether you are going to author your life story or let others tell you how the story goes. I invite you to make the choice to live life from your own perspective, despite all of its unexpected events, with purpose and pride. Emerge from victimhood into victory by the power of words and stories. Like any journey, it will have its ups and downs. I gave up on this manuscript many times and then recommitted to completing it. Those fluctuating moments are okay, as long as overall we remain the author of a story we are proud to tell.

So here is the book I never planned to write. Ben believed in it before I did. Thank you, Ben. And just as this accidental, unplanned event took place, it was up to me to transform it into a story I am proud to share. It took a lot of authoring, literal and metaphorical. Now, it is your turn.

PART 1

# Author Why?

CHAPTER 1

# You Have a Story That Drives Your Life—but Are You the Author of That Story?

"You inspired me to get divorced. Thank you."

I was crossing a busy intersection in Manhattan when I turned with a puzzled expression to look at the stranger who uttered this bombshell statement to me. He rushed to explain.

"I heard you speak five years ago, and your speech inspired me. I took action and got divorced."

I was stunned, mainly because I do not speak about divorce or anything remotely close to it. My work and expertise is in customer experience and employee engagement. Somehow, in the middle of a presentation about the need to elevate performance, this man had found his own message, an actual calling, to gain the courage to sever his marriage.

I was stunned. *What? How? What did I say that caused you to do that?* I thought.

But I did not dare ask him out loud. Somehow that felt as if by asking, I would be challenging his decision. I wanted to stay respectful, especially in light of his confidence to share such a moment with me. I simply thanked him and hurried across the street.

But the incident did not leave me. I pondered it for weeks. What had I said that made him decide to get divorced? As I pondered more, I recalled other similar incidents when people quoted from my books and reacted differently from how I intended. I was always puzzled by those responses. How come they didn't get what I was trying to say?

Over time, as this kept happening and I kept wondering, the answer became clearer: It was not what *I* said; it was what *they* heard.

Yet, for all the times people have responded differently from how I intended, I am still befuddled how they didn't get what I was saying. Wasn't I clear?

The answer is not obvious, but it is simple. Listeners take my words and plant them into a different story—their own story. When we read or listen to stories, we're all getting the same words. But we're fitting them into completely different preexisting conditions, beliefs, aspirations, doubts, and hopes. That is how words can morph into something quite different. The words now live in us, in a different story, and support a different life narrative.

We live in stories. Facts are mere bones, a skeleton that is fleshed out by our story. As we experience the facts, we color them, recrafting them as a story. The story gives these facts meaning, infusing purpose into them. The story determines our next course of action. If our aspirations and hopes take a dominant role in coloring the facts, we are most likely to take positive action with courage. If our past failures and disappointments provide the main meat to the facts, the next action is likely to be procrastination, hesitation, and even resignation. The facts are the same. But the story determines the next step and, therefore, the next chapter of our life.

I remember having a conversation with my older son, when I shared with him my joy in being able to save for his future. His reply shocked me. Instead of being grateful, which is what I expected, he said that these savings put pressure on him and caused him anxiety. The sense of debt he felt for using money I earned placed a huge burden on him.

In my mind, the facts were indisputable: a father gives his son money for the future. Our stories—what we make those facts mean—are totally different. My story was one of family relationships, and caused me joy. My son's story was one of responsibility and burden, which caused him stress. Same facts, different stories.

## Listening to Create Our Story

We live in stories, we listen with our stories, and we act on our stories.

As we listen to words, witness actions, or sit in new experiences, it is not the facts we are recognizing. Instead of simply seeing circumstances as they are, our brain is constantly looking to reaffirm our own story . . . our own narrative. Stories are the unique compilation of our experiences, hopes, aspirations, and disappointments that then shape the perception of our own identity and capabilities. These stories then reconfigure the way we perceive new events in our lives. Given certain stories, we will view the next event as an opportunity to grow. But other stories cause us to perceive the same event as affirming our helplessness and our inability to progress. We are listening with a whole story-crafting tool kit that ultimately wraps the facts with our own slant and crafts a story that fits the narrative we want it to. Factors affecting and building that new narrative include:

- **History**. Our past experiences shape the way we listen to new evidence. How we experienced life until now provides a backdrop for any new information and dictates how we process that new input.

- **Values**. Our purpose and what matters to us in this world are another set of lenses that impact our listening. What we do when we encounter a difficult moment or big opportunity is shaped by the values we hold.

- **Emotions**. Our feelings add a dimension of depth to the facts and wrap them with our unique view. Positive emotions may turn a difficult event into a learning moment. Negative ones will turn it into a reaffirming tragedy that can pave the path for the rest of our lives.

- **Opinions**. What others tell us or think of us affects the way we view the future. Positive views about us may shape the way we accept a request as a challenge. Negative perceptions may lead us to see the request as an invitation to fail.

- **Agenda.** Our motivation and what we want to accomplish will shape our perspective on certain facts or events and will shape them to fit those ambitions.

- **Empowerment.** Our sense of empowerment is what causes us to accept or reject facts or events. If we feel empowered, the facts will assure us and inspire us. If we feel disempowered, the facts will reaffirm that.

We listen with all of these pieces that make up our story, and seek to reaffirm it. In their work "Prospect Theory," Professors Daniel Kahneman and Amos Tversky assess the human reaction toward risk and opportunity. In their research, they have proven that the human mind is more likely to focus on minimizing losses than on maximizing new opportunities, even when the probability for each is exactly the same.[1]

We lean toward reaffirming our current state rather than venturing into new opportunities. Research in change management further supports this idea, highlighting how the brain responds to danger or change by engaging in fight-or-flight mode.[2] Again, we tend to confront the unknown and the new with an attitude of staying put, where we are most comfortable.

As human beings, we are trained to survive before we thrive. To survive is to protect the existing, not to venture into new situations. Hence the instinctive reaffirmation of our stories—it's more reassuring that way. Living in a story we repeatedly reaffirm keeps us in a comfort zone. The familiar story always trumps the challenging one, even if the familiar story is painful. It is the devil we know, and the devil we believe in.

## Change Starts with a New Story

In my work launching and supporting over 250 corporate transformations worldwide, I often come across the issue of the internal story. Employees resist a particular proposed change, clinging passionately to the past. Even when the facts clearly contradict their enthusiastic arguments, still they stick by them.

Once, at a major bank undergoing a digital transformation program, I came up against employees resisting new changes. Many teller windows had been closed as a result of customers shifting to online banking and seeking self-service tools, yet bankers persisted in telling their customers not to use the new tools and to keep on coming to them for in-person service. In a tough conversation I had with some of those bankers, they complained about the lack of respect the new strategy engendered with regard to their contribution to the bank's success. They could not envision a bank without tellers. The fact that customers demanded the new tools and that there was a sharp decline in usage of the tellers, and cash in general, was irrelevant to them. The facts made clear that the role of a bank in customers' lives was shifting dramatically. Yet they insisted that the bank must keep things the way they were.

Confronting these bankers with the hard data was useless. Their stories of the past superseded the numbers. Their stories held strong sway over their convictions, preventing them from seeing the evolving reality.

This was not an isolated case. The employees I worked with at many different companies held onto their life stories time and time again, refusing subconsciously—and sometimes consciously—to evolve by considering new information.

I was trying to get these bankers and tellers to accept a new story, only the stories did not coexist well and hence, the rejection. Only when I softened the process from story dissemination to story co-creation and the development of new listening tools did we start to see evident change. Employees needed to have their story respected, and they also needed to play an integral part in the evolution of a new story. Facts were almost irrelevant to the process (almost).

As I discuss in my book *Next Is Now!*, change resilience is the core competence of the future. I define it as the speed and scope to which we adapt to the new and the unknown. For some, the words *change* and *resilience* do not belong together, which is exactly my point. Resilience belongs to those who can adapt faster. Change resilience is your ability to develop the muscles of change and respond better (and faster) than others in order to survive and thrive. To do so, we need to develop a new story. More specifically, we need to evolve our story. More importantly, we need to be active authors of our story to be ready for the future so we may define *it* rather than being defined *by* it.

## Who Authors Your Story?

Every good story has a hero, a victim, a difficult moment, and a superpower to save the day. Who are you in your story? The victim . . . or the hero? Do you activate the superpower . . . or wait and hope to be saved?

When you review your life story, what are your primary listening tools? Does your story inspire you or drive you to despair?

Does your story drive you to action or paralyze you to a state of victimhood and inaction?

The answers to these questions have nothing to do with the facts of your surroundings and circumstances. The answers are up to you. Will you author your story, or will you have your story written for you by others? To become the hero, you need to decide. To activate your superpower, you need to aspire to something greater than your own current story. This will not happen by default.

Every moment, we make a choice to be the author and hero of our own story and not merely a supporting character in someone else's story.

The person who opted to get divorced following my presentation did not do it because I said anything about getting divorced or finding new love in your life. He did so because he heard an insight that called him to take charge of his life, to rise and to write his next chapter and not let others do it for him. He listened to the call deep inside that invited him to become the hero of his life.

We hear what our life story wants us to hear. We affirm the layers of the story we have crafted over the years and seek to reinforce it. By doing so, we further plant our lives in familiar soil. But is this story the one we would love to write? Is it bringing out the best in us? Is this story leading us to meaningful fulfillment?

If we are not actively authoring that story, the answer is most likely no. If we do not attempt to author our story and change our listening tool kit, we are living within a story crafted *for* us but not *by* us.

It's time to live our own story. But first, we need to change how we listen.

## CHAPTER 2

# Crafting a Deliberate Story

Did Steve Jobs have a vision and a business plan to own the communication world with iPhones? Did Elon Musk craft a well-described document outlining his future dominance for both electric vehicles and space explorations? Did Jeff Bezos know exactly how he was going to ensure he transformed the e-commerce industry?

The answer across the board with them—and so many other incredibly successful people—is likely not.

The technologies that enabled these men's revolutionary contributions to the world didn't initially exist, and therefore such a vision was highly unlikely. Instead, they were equipped with a conviction that they could do things better, that there was a way to improve on the existing solution, and that conviction drove them toward technology development.

These three businessmen's initial story was not world domination; it was world betterment. What they set out to do was to solve a problem to make the world a slightly better place.

How often have we seen companies declaring their vision only to see them falter and fall short (sometimes way short) of those declarations?

So what is the purpose of even having a vision? Of writing your future story?

In a world that is changing so fast, where technologies are transforming whole industries and people's lives in such a radical way, this question is even more relevant than ever before. I would argue that in today's fast-paced changing world, the best path forward is to remain open-minded and uncommitted so you are able to see opportunities without vision blinders. It will help you capture the unimaginable as opposed to pursuing limited, dated visions.

## Redefining Vision: Being Deliberate

It is true that life is moving fast, and today's vision may miss tomorrow's opportunity. But living without vision is far worse. Total openness to anything and everything may result in perpetual indecisiveness and misalignments between who you are, what you can do, and the path you want to pursue.

Vision is not a prescription. A vision does not detail your path for the next fifty years. A vision outlines a path and defines it based on who you are and what you are capable of. Like bumpers in bowling, it should eliminate the wrong path as opposed to defining all the right paths.

In short, you need to have a deliberate—but not detailed— path to realize your vision.

A deliberate vision consists of four components: direction clarity, competence recognition, efforts commitment, and values definition. Together, these four components will create a definition of the vision's direction that you should pursue as well as what other alternatives you should avoid in order to stay focused. This approach will help you to capture the right opportunities and enhance the impact you can create in the world. Let's dive into each one.

- **Direction clarity**. Where would you like to be in the near and far future? Where would you feel most purposeful? Will you be working in medicine, arts, education, sports, production, service, hospitality, industrial design? There are endless choices. Be clear about where you want to be. Eliminate the rest. Being deliberate is being able to see a better future and know what general direction to pursue to get there.

  ◦ In what space or industry do you want to make a difference? Write it down.

- **Competence recognition**. I may want to be an NBA superstar, but my competence will not support this effort. It does not mean my goal is impossible; it means that it is highly improbable. As I once said to my kid's teacher, "I would rather focus on moving him from a B+ in math to an A+ than to focus on his C- in history. He is more likely to become the best mathematician rather than a mediocre historian." It makes more sense to work with your strengths than try to perfect your natural flaws. Your direction should align with the areas where you're most competent.

  ◦ Where do your strengths lie? What can you do that no one else can? Write it down.

- **Efforts commitment**. In my early years, I admired the statement, "If you can dream it, you can do it." It took some hard experience throughout the years to realize that the quote was missing a critical component. It should really say, "If you can dream it and are willing to put in the required effort, you have a better chance of doing it." Dreams without commitment or effort are useless. Be honest with yourself. What price are you willing to pay to reach your deliberate vision? What are you willing to give up to pursue it? No real achievement is gained without effort and paying the price. You are probably not able to realize the full scope of the required commitment, but you can at least recognize that it's not a "dream it, do it" kind of magic. Recognize the struggles up front and be ready to dedicate your efforts.

  ◦ How much are you willing to invest and commit to bring this vision to life? Write it down.

- **Values definition**. Some people will be ruthless in their pursuit of their vision. Others will refuse to compromise their ethical code. Some will insist on using their values to achieve their vision. What are your values? How would they serve you on the journey in that direction?

  ◦ What are your uncompromised values that will guide your vision fulfillment? Write them down.

You now have the beginnings of your deliberate vision.

This doesn't mean you shouldn't still be open to exploring new possibilities, technologies, and opportunities. But it will help you to narrow down and select what you want to pursue.

Having a vision will likely help you to be successful because it describes who you are, where you want to go, the price you are willing to pay, and the value system you bring with you.

## Intentionally Human—the Way We Make a Real Difference

There is a growing industry of art-focused artificial intelligence generators that create images based on humans' commands. Some argue that this is the end of art and artists as we know it because now everyone can become an artist without lifting too many fingers.

Well, some were saying the same thing when photography was invented. The art world is alive and kicking today because it incorporated the photography world into it. If art is merely the practice of putting paint on canvas, it might one day be performed by machines. But if art is an intentional human vision used to convey an emotion and being put to practice through efforts and hard work, then it is indispensable.

When humans live with intentional visions, they create the impossible. AI art is a replication based on billions of original ideas created by original artists crafting original art. It tries to mimic human effort and vision. Let's not confuse the two. When you want to live as an original with a unique promise for this world, live a deliberate vision for your life.

*What is your deliberate vision?*

## CHAPTER 3

# Living the Fake Story—
# Can You Overcome
# Impostor Syndrome?

It was pitch dark at four p.m. in November, in Finland.

I remember waiting in a conference room at a glass office building in Espoo, less than an hour's drive from Helsinki. My anxiety was at its highest, and I noticed that the room was designed in a minimalist way. This meant there were no conference call devices in the room.

I was there to meet the president of Nokia. At the time, Nokia controlled 43 percent of the mobile phone market worldwide. This Finnish conglomerate had succeeded in transforming itself from a company that sold televisions, boots, and wood to becoming the world leader in the emerging marketing of cell phones, outdoing the pioneer of the industry, Motorola. They were a huge success story, an unexpected hero from a land not known for technological leadership.

And here I was to discuss my ideas with the president.

The anxiety overwhelmed me to the point of near paralysis. *Do I really have something new to tell him? Doesn't he have access to top-notch consultants and advisors? What if he says my ideas are stupid or that they thought about them already? What if he dismisses me outright?* All I wanted was for this meeting to be over before it even started. What had I gotten myself into? Why was I here? I thought he might think in the first five minutes that I was a fake. I was terrified.

These thoughts were not new. When I was in front of audiences evangelizing customer experience in the early days when no one was speaking about it, similar emotions would take over and control my thoughts. They were terrifying and paralyzing. It took tremendous efforts to overcome them and go on stage to deliver my message.

Struggling with those thoughts was common for me, but the worst part was that I was scared to share them with anyone. The shame I felt weakened me and often discouraged me from reaching higher.

When my first book didn't perform as I expected, I used this lackluster performance as proof that my negative thoughts were correct. When I would receive a rejection, I would immediately file those rejections in the affirmation drawer, further strengthening my fears of being discovered as a fake.

Later in my life, I discovered that I wasn't alone.

In fact, there was a name for this phenomenon: impostor syndrome. The concept was first described by Pauline R. Clance and Suzanne A. Imes from Georgia State University in a 1978 article entitled "The Impostor Phenomenon in High Achieving Women: Dynamics and Therapeutic Intervention."[1] It describes the psychological phenomenon of a person doubting their skills and accomplishments and living in a state of fear of being exposed as a fraud.

Those who experience impostor syndrome tend to live in a story separated from the facts. They will discount their skills and accomplishments and declare them a matter of luck. They will compare themselves to others and see their performance as inferior. If a sign of success appears to distort their sense of fraud, they will immediately attribute it to external factors such as luck, help from others, or a one-time success. By doing so, they will reaffirm the broader story they live in, which is that they are not as capable as people believe they are.

Research shows that this syndrome is prevalent among women, who often attribute success to teamwork and external factors, while men attribute success to their own skills and capabilities.

As I discovered this phenomenon, I was still ashamed of my thoughts. Even though the condition had a name, I still failed to acknowledge it, address it, or lessen the emotional burden it imposed on me. I was living in that story and didn't let anything penetrate it or change it.

After I met with the Nokia president, I was invited to conduct a workshop for senior executives at the company. The meeting was a success. The president liked my ideas and found them important enough to share with his top executives. And yet, I was left wondering, what was so special in what I had said? Why had he liked my solutions? I was sure that although he hadn't caught my fraudulent persona, one of his executives would certainly expose me. But that never happened. In fact, the workshop led to a series of engagements with Nokia.

The facts were quite different from the story that ran in my head and filled my body. Time and time again, people appreciated and commented on the inspiring nature of my messages. But my head was running a story that was directly influenced by my emotional listening lens. It completely clouded the facts and enveloped them with a shade of doubt that led to anxiety. I wasn't facing the facts, which were the real story of my life. I was living a distorted story highly colored by the dark shadow of negative emotions.

## Removing the Impostor Story— Authoring the Authentic Story

The reasons we develop impostor syndrome are unclear. I believe that most of us experience this anxiety at one point in our career or life. We get this sense of anxiety that we are not qualified for what we are about to perform. The impact of impostor syndrome can be debilitating. It leads some people to depression and others to simply not enjoy what they are doing, as they are too busy thinking about their fears and how to contain them. Even if success hits them in the end, they will discount it and seek affirmation that it was merely a fluke instead of giving themselves credit.

Under the impostor story lies a true story ready to be discovered.

This is a classic case of living in the wrong version of the real story, a story we didn't author deliberately. This collection of negative emotions, from inferiority complex to low self-esteem, can easily lead us to reach this point of defaulting to the wrong version of the real story. These emotions take hold of our perception of reality and shape it into a painful version that directly impacts the quality of our work and life. When we feel a victim of emotions beyond our control, this is exactly when the emotions write our story. The outcome is a story of paralysis, which stops us from reaching higher and thriving in life.

We need to write a new story, one rooted in reality and not emotion.

The good news is, there are several tools we can use to rewrite the story.

## Impostor Syndrome Distorts the Truth

To start reauthoring this story, we need to first be aware of our thoughts and the way they lead us astray. Recognize the pattern and also the burden it imposes. You need to catch those thoughts as soon as they emerge and then realize that they are affecting you. Be in the moment and call impostor syndrome what it is. Don't just try to dismiss thoughts of being a fraud, but label them so you can address them better. Know that you are not alone; many people have experienced feeling like an impostor.

To overcome or at least reduce impostor syndrome, consider the following questions:

- What skills and experience do you possess that are relevant to the role you're doing?

- What impact do you make on people when you execute this task?

- What feedback have you received that is relevant to doing this role better?

- What tools or assistance would help you deliver this role better?

- In what ways can you meet or exceed the objectives of the role?

- What can you do to reduce the risk of failure?

- Why do you think you may fail more than others? (You won't!)

The more you focus on execution and getting equipped to get the job done, the more you will divert the anxiety associated with impostor syndrome into productive channels of success.

## Your Role Is Real

Know that your contribution to a project's achievements and success is real if the facts dictate as much. Recognize that you are a positive addition, even if in a small way, as the right person at the right time to help make the project a success.

If you're not sure whether you're contributing, start a list of your inputs at the onset of the project. This can range from project management, to helping shape the vision of the project, to counting the measurable results. Be clear about your additions and do not belittle any piece of them. No contribution is too small. And no, don't believe your part in the project would have necessarily been brought, seen, or done by others. You saw it.

You called it. You did it. This is your real role in this project, your contribution. Every role matters and every job makes a difference to ensure success.

## The Impact You Make on People Is Real

Instead of just evaluating your skills and accomplishments from your own perspective, review their impact on others. In all my books, I argue that viewing life through the lenses of the recipients of our work often provides us with true appreciation of the impact we create. If people are left feeling inspired, delighted, appreciative, motivated, satisfied, and expressing gratitude, then we have touched them. Those expressions are the mirror to our efforts and creativity. They demonstrate the impact we can create and, better yet, should inspire us to keep going.

If you do not have direct contact with customers, look to your colleagues or family members as recipients of your actions, and examine your impact through their eyes and experiences. Seek feedback from them, and specifically ask how your actions affected them. Seeing your success through the eyes of the recipients can be rather empowering and enlightening. You will be surprised at how small acts you probably took for granted meant much to others. Why? Because you fulfilled a need for them.

## Embrace (Don't Dismiss) the Compliments

When someone is sharing their appreciation, don't sit there terrified and thinking, "Here comes the 'but . . .'" Often there is no "but," just sheer appreciation. And even if there is no "but," we tend to dismiss compliments as coming from someone just being courteous who didn't mean it. That's not a way to live. If you did something of significance—and remember, significance is in the eye of the beholder—then there is no reason to dismiss a person's genuine gratitude. Let this gratitude sink in. Embrace it. Absorb it. Let it refuel you and dilute the negative impostor thoughts. The best antidote to those negative fraud thoughts is positive thoughts of gratitude coming from people you have touched and impacted.

## Un-fake It to Become Real

It's not easy. After years of dismissing our power and impact, claiming everyone else could have done it just as well, seeing the beauty of our work and discovering the real story hiding behind the mask of negative emotions and low self-esteem is difficult. I still struggle too, with pausing and listening to compliments. But I work at trying to allow them to soothe the anxiety and let my narrative be shaped to the real story. I make the effort because I know that living with the fear of being a fraud doesn't help anyone. I don't enjoy it. People are not getting my best performance, and overall, everyone loses.

One of my little tricks you can employ is keeping "thank you" emails and reviewing them in times of doubt. They help to reauthor my story in the moment and gain the power to bring my best to the next challenge.

I have never discussed these thoughts before; they were part of my anxiety and shame. I decided to share them here to hopefully help you reevaluate the power that an impostor story can have on you. The impostor story is not the real story of you. It is being authored by default because you are not taking care to author the real narrative. You are discounting aspects of your real story (such as accomplishments and positive feedback) and letting emotions fill in the blanks instead. It is a classic case of listening with a negative listening lens, amplified by the historical listening lens of someone in the past who dismissed your skills and deflated your motivation. Take those lenses out of the story and reshape it to stand on the true facts, which are your skills, your accomplishments, and the feedback you receive from others. Those are the true components of your story that will allow the real you to shine through.

> *Who would you really be*
> *without the impostor fear?*

## CHAPTER 4

# Are You at the End
# of Your Story . . .
# or Just the Beginning?

How many of your values will change in the next ten years? How many of your values have changed in the last ten years?

Think about this for a moment: did the COVID-19 pandemic change your answers?

The first two questions were at the center of a research project conducted by psychology professor Dan Gilbert of Harvard University. I ask the third to help you further think critically about a recent event that might have changed your long-held values and priorities.

I came across Professor Gilbert's TED Talk several years ago as I worked on my last book about embracing change, *Next Is Now!* Gilbert was attempting to understand our readiness to change and adapt as we go along in life. The operating assumption was that the willingness or ability to predict change will decline over the years and we will be change resistant as we grow older. The results were quite different. Gilbert discovered that eighteen-year-olds' readiness to change is equal to that of fifty-year-olds. We treat future change with a great deal of resistance while we overestimate the amount of change we have experienced to date. He describes these phenomena as "the end-of-history illusion."

While Gilbert's questions related to a change in values, the research results indicated a simple yet surprising truth: we humans tend to underestimate the scope of change that is yet ahead of us. We are inclined to believe that we have already learned most of what there is to learn and are far more prepared for the future than we truly are (hence, my third question). As such, our capacity to deal with future changes is limited to our past experience and is likely to not be sufficient to welcome the unknown future. As Gilbert concludes in his TED Talk, the end-of-history illusion illustrates that we as human beings act as if we are a finished product while we are still a work in progress, and probably will be in such a state until we die.[1]

I was fascinated by the study, as it reaffirmed much of my own qualitative research work around people's readiness to change and adapt. Working with employees of diverse companies, I often found the reluctance to change and evolve was rooted deeply in people's belief that the past is the most accurate representation of the present. Employees act as if they have maximized their capacity to change and none is left for the future.

The result was often one of several predictable paths. The

first path was active resistance or refusal to change, which resulted in dismissal from the organization. Companies refused to allow those employees to hijack the future in the name of their nostalgic past. These active resisters ended up frustrated, bitter, unemployed, and often irrelevant in the marketplace.

The other path was that of the reluctant-to-change employees. They did change but reluctantly, complaining all the way through. Their change was often too little, too late, and represented only the bare minimum required. As a result, the organizations they worked at failed to capture the potential that the change represented and often suffered financially and strategically as a result. The reluctant-to-change employees eventually ended up departing the organization, further affecting the organization's bottom line.

In all those cases, the listening lens of the past clouded the employees' judgment. The facts that supported the change's scope and speed morphed into big threats to be protected from or fought against. What others saw as a beautiful future, resisters viewed as a story of destruction of past achievements. It resulted in those employees living according to the end-of-history illusion. Again, same facts but different stories.

Our love affair with our past might try to control our perspective of the future. Despite the mountain of books about the importance of adapting to change, we continue to ignore this wisdom. We hold onto the past and turn it into the beacon of our future. This dangerous listening lens places us in an increasingly irrelevant position and risks our future. This history-tinted view forces the facts into a preconceived story and forces the story of our life to stand still and refuse to evolve.

## It Is the Story, Not History

I was once approached by an academic institution that was suffering from a decline in donations. They asked me to advise them on how to increase their engagement with donors. Throughout the years, they had produced tens of thousands of alumni who were spread all over the country, many of whom used to donate to the university but were now concentrating their support on other institutions.

I started with the following question:

*On a scale of 1–10, how would you estimate the change that your alumni have experienced in their profession in the last ten years?*

The aggregate result was 9 out of 10.

*On a scale of 1–10, how much change would your alumni face in the next ten years?*

They responded half-jokingly with 12.

*On a scale of 1–10, how much did your curricula evolve in the last ten years or will evolve in the next ten years?*

They embarrassingly responded: 3.

"Here lies the answer to your question," I declared. "You don't have a donor decline issue. You are facing a relevance issue."

I explained to the board members that they were losing relevance because their story refused to shift to consider the major changes their alumni were facing.

"You insist on teaching concepts and skills that are losing relevance in the marketplace at a fast pace," I explained. "As a result, your donors see no reason to support your academic institution. It is not that your donors left you. It is that you left your donors by sticking to your past and refusing to adapt to the future."

Once upon a time, this school's story was fresh and relevant. Their donors were excited and interested in being part of that story. As time changed and relevance evolved, they let their narrative remain history-tied, therefore future-irrelevant.

This is a common practice in academia, especially with the concept of tenure built into the system. Older, once-accomplished professors become stagnant in their thinking and repeat their old formula for success. The tenure process prevents new, fresh perspectives from penetrating academia's walls. Respect for the elders takes precedence, and they lead the way forward with ever-growing-old tools and concepts.

"Marketing techniques are not the solution in your case," I said to the wide-eyed board. "You need to reinvent the story, the core value of the institution. To achieve that, you ought to shed the history-listening lens and tell a future-embracing story, delivered by professors who are excited about guiding their students through the future. This is the way to regain relevance and, eventually, donors."

Such suggestions in academic institutions—and for that matter, successful organizations—are nothing short of heresy. You are often considered disrespectful of the past achievements of the organization and lack the right to suggest future paths. The protection of the past is so ingrained that it clouds the facts and causes many to ignore them or subject these facts to the old way of thinking.

As you consider reinventing the old ways, consider the following questions:

- How many of your values will change in the next ten years?

- How many of your values have changed in the last ten years? (Yes, these are the same questions from the top of the chapter but now carry a different meaning.)

- What surprising life events or challenges have you encountered in the past and conquered?

- What did you learn from those events?

- How did conquering those events prepare and strengthen you to be able to face the future better?

- How can you find excitement in the promise that is included in the unknown future?

Let's find the hidden excitement in the unpredictable. Let us welcome the beauty it will uncover in us. If we already fear the endurance of these events' pain, we might as well be ready to see the rays of beauty they bring with them. By embracing the unpredictable's arrival and welcoming its surprising presence, we assume an intentional state to author the next chapter of our story and take an author seat into the future.

## The Predictable Past and the Unknown Future

What is beautiful about the past is that we know it. We know how it feels and what it looks like. We know how to handle it. We did it once before and we gained all that hindsight wisdom. We are ready for the past to repeat itself. If we can only ensure that history will repeat itself, we will be all good. But it doesn't. Not in the way we hope.

That is why we are inclined to look for shreds of history in the future. We seek to bend the future into our historical perspective and hope that it will equip us with better ways to handle it, manage it, survive it—whatever term you apply.

While history does come with lessons, it does not indicate the future.

History makes us resilient. History makes us smarter. History makes us more confident, as we are armed with the knowledge that we were able to handle challenges in the past.

But history does not make the unknown more known.

History does not make the future less different or distinct.

History does not make the butterflies in the stomach disappear as we face new and exciting challenges.

We need to learn to apply the historical wisdom to strengthen our character but not to distort our evaluation of future opportunities. We ought to not view our life as an end of history and stop all future evolution.

Let history strengthen our identity but not rob us of the excitement of our future.

*What personal historical event is shaping your story?*

## CHAPTER 5

# Who Is Your Hero?
# What Are Your Chances
# of Becoming One?

"Who is your hero?"

I usually ask this question during my presentations about personal excellence.

People love to share their stories about their heroes, and the answers are always fascinating . . . and predictable.

The answers range from Michael Phelps and Michael Jordan to Winston Churchill and Mother Teresa. In between, you will find Gal Gadot, Simone Biles, Wayne Gretzky, Nelson Mandela, Lionel Messi, Usain Bolt, Taylor Swift, Maya Angelou, Sir Alex Ferguson, Paul McCartney, Abraham Lincoln, Mark Zuckerberg, Britney Spears, Vanessa Williams . . . and the list goes on.

I say the answers are predictable because for audiences worldwide, most of the responses cite legends, celebrities, famous athletes, or politicians. Our pictures of excellence, and for that matter heroes, are very specific.

What do all these heroes have in common? They have reached an outsized achievement by making a huge personal sacrifice for the betterment of the world, or they have accomplished some world record.

Our heroes are people who have lived extraordinary lives where a huge sacrifice was an integral part of their existence. Their ambition or response to a world's problem was out- sized as well.

In short, they weren't normal like you and me. They were the exception to the rule, more legend than human. They lived in pursuit of an out-of-this-world goal that 99.9 percent of the world population would never dream of, let alone attempt to achieve.

Based on these examples, heroes are (for most people) more legend than human.

Heroes are unlikely to be you and me.

One of the lessons I learned about heroes is that the way we define them often dictates if we will ever choose to become one.

When we associate heroes with bigger-than-life characters who made a major sacrifice to achieve an outsized accomplish- ment, we often don't include ourselves as hero material. We simply exclude ourselves from the possibility. After all, if a hero is someone who wins twenty-eight Olympic medals as Michael Phelps has done, I have no chance. I won't even try.

The rare few that usually answer "my mom" or "my teacher" during my presentation are the ones who realize that heroes are people with talent and motivation who respond differently during a time of opportunity. When a crisis happens, they don't run from it or wait for someone to save them. They see an invitation to rise and gather all their talent toward a solution.

## Rethinking Our Heroes

When you read stories, the heroes usually do not carry a sense of mission to save the world. They discover it as an opportunity that presents itself. In many stories, the heroes are reluctant. But they never excuse themselves from responsibility and the possibility of a better world.

Real heroes do not wear T-shirts declaring that they're heroes. They don't even know they are heroes, as they are deep in the process and pursuit of some sort of greatness.

So how did we develop the celebrity-admiring version of heroes?

We distorted the hero definition. We placed a huge light on the hero's moment of achievement without acknowledging or even seeing all the sweat, pain, effort, failures, trials, and errors that came before.

When Simone Biles bowed out of the Olympics in Tokyo to take care of her mental health, she shocked the world. She was the top contender, expected to win many medals. Yet, the expectations from her were enormous and borderline inhuman. What Simone Biles ultimately did is prioritize herself as a human being first. She was not a medal-producing legendary hero, but rather a human attempting to rise up to new achievements and, in the process, experiencing pain and difficulties. She displayed the human version of heroism, not the legendary version.

I remember flying through Chicago O'Hare airport and seeing her posters hanging everywhere, highlighting the great expectations of the athletic hero Simone Biles. These posters didn't tell the story of Simone Biles the human being, and she decided to be human first. It wasn't the medals that made her a hero, but her immense courage.

Real heroes are humans first who manage to achieve great things. They are not great achievements that happen to be humans.

## Discovering the Hero That You Are

Every day is an opportunity to become heroic, if we only include ourselves in the definition or possibility of becoming a hero. We all have talent that is relevant in a certain time of opportunity. Everyone has a hero inside them, waiting to be uncovered. We all need to choose to develop and nurture this talent so it will be ready at the right moment, when a need and opportunity to be heroic arises.

There really is a hero in all of us. Heroes are not their glory moments when they are on the podium and the flag is waving while the national anthem plays in the background. We need to start to see these people in a fuller, more human way that includes their journey to get there—the same kind of journey you might take.

To discover the hero within you, consider the following questions:

- When others describe you, what would they say is your best quality?

- What kinds of situations have led to you "saving the day"?

- What is the superpower that, when you use it, you feel full of energy?

- When are you in the "zone"?

- What do you consider your gift to the world?

We all came with gifts to give. Sometimes we don't recognize them or flat-out dismiss them, which is why oftentimes others will know them better than us. That's because what we might see as ordinary, others might see as a power they've learned to count on. Start with discovering that power and the impact it makes on others. When you choose to activate it, that power can become heroic.

Becoming a hero starts at the moment of decision. Heroes don't decide to become heroes but rather determine to refine their skills, nurture their talent, and execute on everyday greatness to become hero-worthy. All your heroes have had that moment. It might have emerged out of a difficult time or one of inspiration. They might have seen someone suffering or someone rising. Then they decided, "One day, that will be me."

It is at that moment that heroes are first born. Later, they merely execute on that decision to rise. The moment we decide to execute on our gifts—to use our superpowers, to become proactive—is hidden from others' eyes. It is a private moment for each one of us.

Then comes the long journey of refining and preparing ourselves for the moment of opportunity. That journey is not pretty and is full of ups and downs, trials and failures. Most people don't see this part of the voyage. The truth is, many accomplished individuals do not spend much time telling their effort stories—but they should.

The story of the journey is far more human, relevant, and accessible. That is where you will find that your hero is not an overnight twenty-gold-medal Olympian, but rather a person like you who opted to use their time and talent differently. They chose to answer the call and pay the often-unexpected price required to get there. The hero emerged in moments of courage to push forward when the chances were slim, not in victory on the podium. If you want to be inspired and become your own hero, simply take the journey and you will find yourself there.

We are all blessed with talent. We all have times and opportunities where this talent is needed and in high demand, with people on the other side benefiting from our decision to execute. It is up to you to be a hero, if you are willing to go through the challenging journey to be ready to answer the call.

*What is your superpower that drives your courage?*

## CHAPTER 6

# Good News or Bad News First? What Your Answer Says about You

"I have good news and bad news. Which one do you want first?"

What would you answer?

I posted this question in a recent presentation to over three hundred people via a Zoom presentation. They were asked for the thumbs-up emoji to indicate good news first and the shocked face emoji if they preferred the bad news first.

Over 75 percent chose the bad news first.

I repeated the experiment in another presentation with similar results where only a small majority preferred the good news first.

Why does this matter? Because your preference for bad news or good news indicates the perspective you have on life.

Good news–first people view the world as a set of opportunities to seize and explore. They view themselves as empowered individuals who are there to explore and expand on the opportunities in life. They feel empowered and ready. They are creators of the new and exciting. They see the world as full of promise and regard problems as small obstacles on the way to a better future.

Bad news–first people are fixers. The world is a series of problems in need of fixing, and they are ready for the next firefight. Their sense of empowerment is limited. They constantly catch up to the world's problems and do not see a horizon of a better future ahead of them. Instead, they focus on plugging the holes. The future is accidentally happening while they are mending the world.

This approach to life demonstrates the dominance of past disappointments in their life's story. As such, they view the facts as a continuation of previous problems waiting to be fixed as opposed to new opportunities for growth and development. Again, the color we add to the facts drives our next course of action.

Over time, we become less like dreamers and more like firefighters. We're ready for the fires instead of dreaming about the opportunities. We all have disappointments from our past, and mostly we don't alter how we perceive life events as a result of those disappointments. They remain scars that reshape our lens to seek out trouble instead of opportunities. Firefighters want bad news first. Those open wounds we failed to heal inform us that everything is bad, so we might as well bring on the bad news and fight the fire. We also don't know how to process gratitude; we dismiss it (which I'll get into more in the next chapter). Gratitude is supposed to balance the negative. But we keep it out, so it keeps us in firefighting mode versus looking for opportunities.

I'm guessing you never thought about the simple answer to the question of "good news or bad news first" in this context. I didn't either. I used to be a bad news–first person.

I connected the dots on the depth of this issue while working with one of my managers who always insisted on hearing the bad news first. He regarded himself as a "fixer," as he needed problems to fix. He approached all our work together as a series of problems that needed to be fixed. That was the essence of his contribution to the world. Sometimes I felt like he was creating problems just so he could fix them. Fires were his bread and butter. The more the merrier. One time he flew from Los Angeles to New York on a short twenty-four-hour notice just because he decided that a certain missed target was a project he must tackle immediately. He spent two days analyzing every number possible to try to fix the problem. He came to life when problems arose. He wasn't great, however, at envisioning a better future. He could not see beyond the immediate needs and extend toward a future yet to be created. Every fact was a threat and not an opportunity. In his mind, good news was suspicious and must contain bad news within it yet to be discovered.

His story was, "The world cannot be good. It is bad and needs my firefighting skills to amend it."

Imagine working for this person. What do you think the vibe is around him? What kind of conversations were happening among his peers and employees?

You can probably figure it out. They were living in a constant state of crisis with him as the ultimate redeemer. There was no hope for a better place, a vision for a beautiful tomorrow, or a sense of empowerment for each employee to go and make it happen. Instead, they were trapped in a world of finding or even creating the next crisis.

This approach came with a price. While this manager might have been good at what he did, he never provided me with ideas for growth. He was mostly a "maintain the current performance" kind of guy, not your "let's build a better, more beautiful world" kind of a leader. If I had run the business based on his approach to life, we would never have grown and evolved much.

## Fixer or creator? What do you choose?

Who are you: a fixer or a creator? Do you believe in a better future or in fixing the current state?

Your decision says a lot about you. More importantly, it sets your life's path and authors your story in a certain way.

Some people may argue that the answer is not in their hands. They say it's just who they are, that it's in their nature. Well, I beg to differ.

Being a fixer or creator is not a life verdict. It is a choice. More importantly, it is a muscle that requires training. Your past listening lens might be informing how you decide to show up in the world, but it doesn't mean that you cannot evolve into a person of future possibilities.

Your decision to either fix or create sets your life's path and authors your story in a certain way. Focusing on the fixing first is assuming a listening lens of helplessness and a "world against me" attitude. It comes with constant dissatisfaction and anxiety about where the next problem will arise. It's like playing a constant game of Whac-A-Mole. You never win, and the house always has the upper hand.

Is that really the world perspective and life story you wish to author? If yes, then the good news is that you do not need to author such a life proactively because it will automatically happen. You will become a victim of circumstances, running on a hamster wheel that goes nowhere.

Alternatively, you can decide that life is always bringing something better right around the corner. When you decide to become a creator taking advantage of opportunities, you choose to overcome the obstacles. You don't let them become the story of your life but rather seek to identify opportunities that will create a better world.

That doesn't mean you're delusional. The problems are still there, but they are not the destination. They are milestones, part of the refinement process toward reaching a better future.

The fixer sees the problems as the main course. The creator views them as merely the appetizer of the meal of life.

When discussing this concept and choice with people, I received some pushback. Some people choose bad news first yet still consider themselves to be creators. They claim that their choice for bad news first is to get the bad news out of the way so they can focus on creating the future. If indeed this is their mindset, then they are simply creators with a different priority. But they are creators, nevertheless. If you can handle the bad news not as the main course but as the appetizer, then you are a creator who fixes while creating the future.

To identify your state of mind, consider the following questions:

- What do you seek first, good news or bad news?

- In addressing the news, do you attempt to solve or consult with your colleagues?

- Do you seek their opinions?

- Do you provide tools and empowerment for others to address the news?

- Do you use language of trust or of control?

- Do you invest time in developing your team to address that news in the future?

- Do you paint a beautiful vision for the future and connect the news to that vision?

- In resolving the issue, did you create a new and better solution or merely patch the old way of doing business?

You need to have awareness in the moment to choose to become a creator. It is the critical step toward changing the pattern of bad news first and its behavioral consequences.

## A Simple Question—Deeper Story

Your listening lens is powerful. It can shift your story one way or another. You're probably starting to see how that listening lens informs the way you view circumstances, and therefore the actions you take. If you feel helpless in life, you will view opportunities as threats and will ignore or fight them. If you feel powerful, your story will evolve to a place of creating a better future.

The facts may be the same. But two different people with two different listening lenses will craft them into very different stories. It is not the facts that drive the next course of action and write the next life's chapter; it is the story. The color we wrap the facts in will determine the power of the next chapter in our life's story.

If your mindset is planted in the bad news–first domain, don't worry. You can make a change. To view the world in a new way through a new listening lens, start by focusing on your power.

1. **Identify the power you do have in the situation.** What is the power you bring to addressing the imminent crisis? What makes you qualified to address it?

2. **Examine the crisis and ask yourself: What are the opportunities hidden inside?** If you are already addressing the issue, can you go beyond simply fixing it? Can you create a new reality? Can your solution transcend the current problem and solve future ones?

3. **Apply your power to a bigger-than-fixing solution.** Envision a sustainable solution with new dimensions or benefits and act on it.

4. **Document your success** and recognize the opportunities you have uncovered and realized.

Slowly, as you apply this approach, bad news–first will become good news–first. You will see the potential in every situation to go beyond the crisis mode and find new ways to create a better future. Changing a mindset is not just a matter of deciding to do so. It is all about practicing the decision in a real-life situation. This is how, slowly but surely, you will develop a creator rather than a fixer approach and become the person who welcomes any kind of news as an opportunity to apply power to create a better future.

Now you have a story with a hero—not a victim—ready to create a new chapter. Good luck discovering your power, and then the opportunities.

*Are you a problem fixer or a creator of a better tomorrow??*

## CHAPTER 7

# Our Deepest Fears of Gratitude—Why Can't We Accept Compliments?

S tacey sat down with trepidation, waiting to receive some awful verdict that would change her life forever. But she wasn't among a jury of her peers or even before a judge. She was with me for our annual performance evaluation session.

We were prepared to discuss her performance in the past year and her objectives for the coming year. It is a process we conduct every year, and people are naturally nervous about which way these things are going to go.

What Stacey didn't realize yet was that she had no need to be nervous. She had worked for me for five years and had grown tremendously. She asked all the "stupid" questions because she wanted to understand and was not ashamed to explore. Clients loved her and she took initiative, often expanding her work with us if she was the project manager. She was awesome, and I was ready to tell her as much.

Performance evaluations often provide positive feedback as well as constructive criticism or ideas for improvements. This time I decided to do it differently. I broke the rules and crafted a performance evaluation session full only of positive feedback.

I started to review Stacey's objectives for the past year and provided my assessment of the results with 10s across the board. While I was giving her glowing praise, I noticed that she was growing anxious, and it was clear that she was hardly paying attention to what I was saying.

I figured maybe I wasn't clearly communicating, so I upgraded my terminology with words like "exceptional" and "remarkable" and "awesome," hoping she would hear me out. But these words seemed to have created a countereffect, and her facial expression demonstrated even greater anxiety (bordering on being terrified).

I was puzzled. Hers was a strange response to what I thought would be welcome praise. I paused, then I said, "Is everything okay?"

"Yes," she replied. "I would just rather skip this section and go straight to what I did wrong. The more I hear positive feedback, the more I think that there is something even worse that I have done. Can we just get to the bad news?"

I was startled.

"Wow, I wasn't expecting that," I responded. "Why do you think there is a worse thing coming?"

"Because there always is," she said. "That is why you are showering me with all this praise, to cushion the bad news. So just go ahead with the bad news."

"Well, there is no bad news today," I declared. "Only good news. You were awesome. Keep up the great work. Aside from that, how can I help you grow?"

Silence.

"What's wrong?" I asked.

"I'm not sure what to say."

"Um, 'thank you'?" I suggested.

"Is this for real?"

"Why wouldn't it be?" I was puzzled.

She didn't reply. Instead, she teared up. She finally eked out a "thank you" before going back to her desk.

Stacey went back to being the awesome performer she was like nothing had happened, but I couldn't help but reflect on that discussion for weeks. In further thinking about our work together, I realized that Stacey could not accept compliments. In this instance, she was suspecting that my positive feedback was an insincere mask for some horrible news. In fact, anytime I had given her praise, she had waved it off. She didn't let the positive gratitude reinforce her strengths and refuel her energy. Instead, she let it roll over her.

## Ignoring Gratitude . . . but Why?

I started to investigate this phenomenon and confronted people with the simple question of "What do you do with gratitude and positive feedback provided to you by friends, colleagues, or managers?" I realized many people were suffering from the phenomenon that I call the gratitude denial syndrome. They just hide their denial better than Stacey.

When confronted with positive feedback, we tend to dismiss it and try to rush the conversation. We feel uncomfortable with positive words and do not know what to do with them. But why?

For some of the people I interviewed, the issue was simple: they didn't trust the positive feedback. They felt that the providers of the positive feedback were not sincere. To them, the compliments sounded superficial, inauthentic, or were carrying a hidden agenda. Therefore, they dismissed the feedback as not real and not relevant.

In other cases, while they thought the gratitude was sincere, the dismissal came from old-fashioned values that taught them not to brag or take credit publicly. They would dismiss or assign gratitude to other people, to the team, or to mere luck—to anything or anyone but themselves, the person who did the work and delivered. They felt that it was a more courteous way to handle the situation.

Some argue that there is harm in spreading gratitude to others. If you share gratitude, they claim, employees will become more entitled and demanding. I beg to differ. If you want to share accomplishments with others, do so. It's a noble act, especially if they deserve it. But not at your own expense.

Robbing yourself of positive feedback, gratitude, and praise is denying yourself a critical nutrient needed for your energy. You need to renew your efforts, and to do so, you need gratitude as fuel. We cannot live off a diet of only constructive criticism. Living off "you are never good enough" is an awful way to live and will ultimately break you down. Your energy diet ought to include gratitude nutrients that will soothe the soul and reenergize the spirit. Ignoring, denying, minimizing, and relegating gratitude and positive feedback will be damaging to your future accomplishments.

As you consider your attitude toward gratitude, consider the following questions:

- When was the last time you provided gratitude to someone who deserved it?

- How did the person respond to the expression of gratitude?

- What would you have hoped the person would feel when you expressed your gratitude?

- If they tried to minimize the cause for gratitude or ignored it altogether, how did you feel?

- What could you have done to make your expression of gratitude more impactful?

- How often do people share gratitude with you?

- What is your response to their gratitude?

- If you tend to dismiss it or ignore it, how do you think it makes them feel?

These questions are geared toward helping you rethink the whole experience of sharing gratitude. The negative impact of not accepting gratitude is felt both by provider and recipient. As a provider, after encountering a dismissal, you will likely conclude that there is no point in trying in the future to provide gratitude if people are just ignoring it. It will result in taking many good actions and excellent performance for granted. Not a fun world to live in.

As a recipient, by ignoring or dismissing gratitude, you stop yourself from refueling the goodness in your life. The expression of gratitude is like fuel for reaffirming your beliefs, values, and choices. Ignoring gratitude leaves those beliefs, values, and choices lacking support for future actions. Again, not a fun way to live.

## Overcoming the Fear

We need to overcome the fear that if we accept positive feedback, something bad is waiting right around the corner. This is an example of the emotional listening lens. It is authoring your story in a distorted way, leaving you constantly on edge and robbing you of the rejuvenating moments of pleasure following great accomplishments. These moments are designed to refuel our energy, and you're just throwing them away.

Living with this fear is living in a distorted story. We need to re-author it and stop the vicious cycle of working hard but denying gratitude, focusing instead on the failures.

For those of you who are ready to admit that you may be suffering from gratitude denial syndrome, here is my proposed path forward: Read the poem by Marianne Williamson called "A Return to Love." In it, she has the perspective that our light, our power frightens us more than our inadequacy and darkness. Then she encourages us to be liberated from our fear, which will, in turn, liberate others. Reflect on her words. Identify the beautiful, courageous, innovative, creative, powerful, caring person in you and live to bring these forces to life. When someone gives you a compliment or shares a word of gratitude, pause, smile, say thank you, and reflect. Let the gratitude sink in and refuel your energy. Take a few moments to celebrate. Recognize that you made progress, you reached a milestone, you made an impact on someone. You are a hero. That is how you build your story.

Your story is authored through your actions, and the gratitude expressed is not fake. It is a reflection of success and one of the chapters in the writing of your story. Don't deny or minimize this chapter. Write with pride (not arrogance), and let it be a stepping-stone toward your next accomplishment.

*Why won't you accept words of gratitude as authentic expressions of your performance?*

## CHAPTER 8

# My Truth Confirmed . . . or Is It Just an Opinion?

I magine a world in which everything you say is true . . .

Every idea you utter is immediately embraced by others.

Every joke you tell causes people to burst into tears of laughter.

Your wisdom seems to know and predict the future.

You are the smartest (and funniest) person in the room. All the time.

Life is perfect.

But . . . is it?

Is it exciting when you have only your one-dimensional viewpoint of the world?

Probably not.

It is life without excitement and surprises.

It is life without diverse colors.

It is life without growth.

It is a world where everyone looks like you and thinks like you.

It is boring.

And yet, we are rapidly drifting in that direction.

Let me explain: We've all experienced confirmation bias as we encounter different opinions and ideas. Confirmation bias is the phenomenon by which we view facts through the lenses of our convictions, hypotheses, and agendas. Instead of examining the facts independently, we subject them to our wishes and desires for the reinforcement of our senses of comfort and our beliefs. The phenomenon was first described by Peter Cathcart Wason, a cognitive psychologist at University College, London, who pioneered the psychology of reasoning.[1] However, the phenomenon received a major boost in the last decade from social media technology creators who want to keep our eyeballs glued to their products so they can ultimately sell our attention to advertisers.

In his book *The Listening Revolution*, Yona Goodman describes succinctly that in the world of social media, our attention is the commodity being traded by the social networks to advertisers. We are not consumers, Goodman argues. Our attention is in fact the product being sold.[2] The most effective method to capture this commodity and deliver it to advertisers is to create a social echo chamber in which we no longer listen to the opinions of others, but "upgrade" our own thoughts to absolute truths. This upgrade takes place when we surround ourselves with viewpoints that are similar to ours but sometimes more extreme. This creates a sense that the real world is the world of those opinions and, when reinforced by our own, become upgraded to be perceived as truth. The constant playing and replaying of these truths does not leave room for any opposing thought to enter into our world except for the purpose of direct opposition. We therefore come to live in a world in which we feel that we are always right.

But this perceived truth is not actually the truth. We are crafting a limited (and therefore distorted) view of the world that fits what we like to hear and believe, while we ignore other opinions. Once again, the facts are being wrapped into our own listening lens colors and are becoming our story. Not *the real* story.

If in the past our confirmation bias was based on our own internal convictions, it is now amplified by living communities of like-minded people who refuse to accept different or dissenting opinions. They feel amazingly comfortable in their own confirmation of the "truth." Transforming confirmation bias from an individual experience to a social experience magnifies its effect and strengthens the resistance to listen to the facts independently with an open mind.

Some would argue that living in our own echo chamber is not hurting anyone. Well, think again.

Even before the emergence of the deliberately designed social echo chamber, confirmation bias carried some serious risks.

Imagine your doctor half listening to you describe your symptoms, then giving a diagnosis and prescribing medicine. It's the same medicine he prescribed to other patients with similar symptoms, but your condition is different than theirs. Your doctor, however, was counting on his experience in hundreds of similar cases over listening to your specific case and treating it individually. What are the chances that this doctor has prescribed you with the wrong treatment?

A 2017 Mayo Clinic study found that only 12 percent of patients seeking a second opinion had been diagnosed correctly by their primary care physician. The doctors offering the second opinion reported that 80 percent of the patients who searched for a second opinion ended up with a new diagnosis.[3] I have no doubt that the first round of doctors were trying their best. But there is a good chance that some of them fell into the confirmation bias trap and delivered a diagnosis that fit their past pattern of experience rather than one that fit the case in front of them.

Research on the impact of confirmation bias in courthouses demonstrated that judges and jurors may fall into the same trap and may view defendants with a biased perspective based on their past convictions.

Confirmation bias, individual or shared, limits our ability to author the real story. It is often driven by an agenda, such as wanting to sound intelligent, refusing to change previous decisions so as not to appear "wrong," selecting the easy path forward, and avoiding challenging work (just to name a few). Confirmation bias leads us to view the facts with a listening lens that does not reflect the true nature of these facts and the opportunities (or threats) that they possess.

## "Maybe. I do not know. Let's examine the facts."

Professor Kevin Kaiser commonly responded with this phrase during a course I took at Wharton School of Business at the University of Pennsylvania. Despite decades of experience, the one truth he was convinced of is that he is not sure. His approach forced him to follow a diligent, disciplined methodology to examine the facts and then draw conclusions. While I do not remember many of the concepts taught offhand, this built-in doubt was the real gift I took from his course.

To overcome confirmation bias, we ought to adopt a deliberate and active approach to questioning what otherwise will be presented to us as truth. The listening lenses of agenda powered by confirmation bias will lead us to make some serious mistakes and reach vastly different conclusions.

Awareness is the first step toward combating these rather ingrained listening lenses. Even if you are pursuing an agenda, make sure you are aware of the high likelihood that you will approach facts with a distorted bias.

As you seek to develop a more balanced approach toward analyzing information to minimize confirmation bias, consider the following questions:

- Can you make the argument for the other opinion before deciding to take a certain position?

- What voices and opinions do you ignore today that would add to your collective thinking process?

- What assumptions do you make when confirming your truth?

- What paradigm guides your convictions?

- How long have you been holding that paradigm?

- What changes in the world may challenge that paradigm?

- What is the price of being wrong?

- What beauty may be in trying something new for just a little bit?

Our thinking gets fixed over time, with convictions and paradigms assuming the world is singularly dimensional and not evolving. But so many aspects of life evolve faster than we are willing to admit, and it is convenient to simply stick to the old, comfortable paradigms rather than explore the truth as it evolves. There is a price we pay when we stay still while the train of life is speeding by. If we are honest with ourselves, life becomes too predictable and boring.

A fast-growing US insurance company challenged me with creating an innovation optimization model. The problem we were addressing was an idea overflow. The company did not have the resources to pursue all the ideas proposed by employees.

To address this, I developed a ten-dimension decision optimization model with them. To evaluate the model, we conducted workshops where executives were asked to evaluate different pending innovation ideas considering the new model. They then needed to decide which innovation requests to assign resources to and which ones to let go.

The interesting insight for this workshop was that when applying the ten-dimension decision model to those ideas, some of the ardent cheerleaders of those ideas abandoned them. They recognized that their enthusiasm for a certain idea was based on one or two dimensions. When examined in its entirety, the idea was not that good. They were incredibly surprised to see how poorly some of their beloved ideas scored.

Once you've started adopting awareness, design a simple decision criterion that will force you to evaluate facts with an open mind. Explore opposing ideas and facts to make sure that you can see the full picture of possibilities and opportunities. There is a cost if you don't rid yourself of confirmation bias.

Consider the following questions:

- By continuing past success due to the confirmation bias, what opportunities would you miss?

- Is extending the past success a feasible option?

- If yes, for how long?

- Considering the dynamic nature of life, is confirming past success in a shifting environment the right decision?

- What if there were different versions of success?

- Why is being attached to your version of success so important to you?

In Entrepreneurship 101, my younger son was taught that "startups fail; entrepreneurs do not." I liked the sentiment. It actually goes to a deeper insight about success and failure. People often equate their achievements or success with their identity. As such, their identity is linked to what they have accomplished, not who they are. The risk with this approach is that the moment they face challenging times, their identity takes a beating. It weakens their ability to cope with those challenges.

While success and identity are linked, they are not interdependent. Our success is what we did, and our identity is who we are. You are not only the sum of your achievements or failures. They are building blocks, but they are not you. Therefore, confirmation bias doesn't protect our identity; it is merely retelling the story of one outcome we achieved in the past.

Confirmation bias is a natural outcome of human experience. We love our success. We get attached to our viewpoints.

We defend our opinions. All this passion inside us is human. But we ought to be careful not to transform every opinion of ours into truth.

Our evaluation of opportunities and threats should be equally balanced, and not influenced by our past fears or our glorified aspirations. Our experience is always valuable in selecting a path forward, but not in assessing the facts. We need to distinguish between the two. The story of our life should be authentic to the facts we are facing. It is the best way to make the most out of opportunities and remove our biggest fears.

*What opportunities do you miss*
*by confirming the status quo?*

## CHAPTER 9

# Authoring the Unknown

How do you write a story you do not know?

You do not know the end game of your story.

You do not know the milestones on the journey.

You do not know the time frame of your story.

You do not know all the actors in your story.

You do not know all the geographical backdrops for your story.

The only thing you know for certain is the character that is yourself. Even that character may surprise you.

This is not going to be an easy story to author. But in many ways, the unknown is what will make it powerful, surprising, and inspiring.

If you ever hear novelists speak about their process, you will discover that they split into two categories. The first group are those who know the plot from the start, and the writing process is merely a documentation of the story they envision in their imagination. Writing for them is like painting a picture with all the images already drawn in pencil, and they just need to add color and bring the picture to life. In this case, the words are acting as the colors.

The second school of authors goes on a discovery journey. Their story is not fully defined, and the endgame (as well as the twists and turns of the plot) is yet to be discovered. In fact, many of these authors describe their writing process as that of discovery, in which they invent their characters and the plot as they go. While they have a general direction of where they are heading, they do not have a full outline and let the creative process lead the way. More than just the plot is unknown. The characters are also being defined and tweaked. This author's craft is the equivalent of putting color on a canvas without the pencil outlines. They wait and see where it will go. Words for them are a form of pure creation, not just colors added to an outline.

Authoring your life story fits more with the second category of authors, but you can apply a little wisdom from the first group. You can author the unknown.

## The Tools to Author the Unknown

Rabbi Jonathan Sacks noted in his writing that in life every person is placed at the juncture between what our skills are and where we are needed the most. He claims that in every situation, we are in a unique individual position to make a difference and leave an impact on the world. Our character and every opportunity or situation we encounter were crafted especially for us to be there and add our special touch. He asserted that human lives are full of purpose, even if we do not know what that purpose is. We came to Earth to fulfill that purpose, and we are given the tools and opportunity to do it. Without us and our purposeful life, the world will not be complete.[1]

This assertion is inspiring for me, especially in the darkest places where I have no idea what is going on, where I feel helpless and without control. In these moments, I remind myself that even without my full knowledge and awareness, I am still where I am needed the most, and I have the tools I need.

The toolbox of our life story consists of four tools: dreams, skills, opportunities, and impact. Together, they create the framework in which we can craft every chapter of our life and make it meaningful. They are truly the tools of authoring the story.

Let us examine them one at a time:

- **Dreams**—Dreams are your outline of the future. Like authors who know the plot from the start, you can outline a future goal and start walking down that path. Dreams guide you to pursue certain careers or relationships. They are the expression of your passion and your hopes.

- **Skills**—Each and every one of us is blessed with unique gifts. From telling good jokes to playing the harp, we each bring a uniqueness that is destined to make a difference, inspire people, and create a unique contribution to the world. Even if you ask different guitar players to play the same tune, each will play it uniquely, reflecting their own nuances and approach to music. These skills, when honed, are primed to respond to the right opportunities.

- **Opportunities**—These are the unique circumstances that we create or find ourselves in. It is the life moments we are presented with where we can make a difference.

Opportunities are, however, not only about time and place, but must be taken advantage of with an awareness and willingness to apply our skills to address the situation in front of us. Sometimes we may be offered opportunities but miss them altogether due to ignorance or a lack of motivation. That is why we need to combine the presence of an opportunity with our own mindfulness at the time to fully capture it.

- **Impact**—The outcome of our actions as experienced by other people is the ultimate impact we create in the world. It can be people who we see and who provide us with feedback, or people on the other side of the world who benefit (or are harmed) by our decisions and actions.

The combination of dreams, skills, opportunities, and impact are the framework for your life story authoring. Dreams can direct you to the right place, where you will then apply your best skills to the right opportunities to make the most unique impact on the world.

## Excellence: A Work in Progress

If you had a chance to purchase an Olympic medal and be declared a winner without the hardship of training, failing, and winning competitions, would you do it?

Most people would say no.

Why? Because without the sweat, hardship, and thrill of competition, it is not worth it. It's fake. What gives the medal and the winning meaning is the hardship that came before it—the pain of losing, the sleepless nights, the tough training, and even the travel to different competitions. Hardship is part of the journey, and without it, you will not care for the "declared achievement." Nothing risked, nothing gained.

This is the essence of real and worthy achievement. The work behind the prize is what makes it valuable, not the actual medal. An Olympic winner starts with dreams but with zero guarantees and plenty of naysayers trying to convince them that they are not good enough. They need the skills and opportunities, and if they win, they will make an impact by inspiring others. But as they start the story of the journey, they are unclear about the story's ending, unsure about the efforts required to complete the mission they accepted, and do not fully recognize the difficulties ahead of them or the talents of the other competitors. Yet they still dream and then take the first step, and then the next. They keep on pursuing the dream until they unfold the story one chapter at a time.

As you are authoring the unknown and seek to remove the fear associated with it, consider the following questions:

- When was the last "unknown" you were involved in, and what was your feeling during the experience?

- What was your attitude going into it?

- If your initial response to the event was of a passive recipient, why was that?

- Did you shift your response from that of a passive, helpless recipient to a powerful, helpful participant?

- What triggered the shift from passivity to action?

- How did you feel as an active participant?

- In retrospect, would you have shifted earlier?

- What did you learn from this experience?

Life is about authoring the unknown. We just need to choose to do so, not as a helpless recipient but to transform into an active participant sooner. Doing so will not make the unknown less unknown, but it will put you in an authoring role, shaping the chapter.

To author your life story, you need to be intentional, determined, and pursue the next steps. Sometimes you will get lucky, but luck is usually an outcome of years of pursuing, trying, failing, and getting up.

## The Impact Pursuit: Are You a Giver or a Taker?

There are two types of protagonists in life stories: the givers and the takers. As children, we grow and take from the world in the form of education, health services, and our parents' efforts, among other things. After we decide on a career path, we start giving back by creating products, services, and experiences that make people's lives better. In the process, we still also consume and take from the world to develop, create, and live. The question is: What is our bottom line? Did we give more than we took or vice versa? Did we replenish what we took and then leave some more?

To be a true-life story author, use impact pursuit as your ultimate compass. Life will throw you an unknown number of curveballs. You will end up in plenty of places and situations you did not want or plan to be in. The ultimate tool in your toolbox will be the pursuit of giving more than you take and a commitment to make a positive impact on the world.

This compass will also help you identify the other tools in your toolbox. It will direct your dreams away from selfishness and toward influencing people. It will help you see your skills and choose to refine the ones that will make a difference. I know you are really good at Candy Crush, but is it really the right skill to develop and spend your waking hours on?

Most of all, with an impact perspective, you will see the opportunities in front of you clearly. They will shine and call upon you to apply your skills in the moment when and where the world (or the people around you) needs you the most. This is how you will author a life story that might yet be unfolding but will make you feel proud and purposeful.

*What is the first defining moment
that started your journey?*

## CHAPTER 10

# The Fear That Drives Your Authoring

When Ethan Katz watched the devastating destruction that Hurricane Katrina brought upon New Orleans, he felt that he couldn't just sit by and watch it. As a director of a youth group in New Jersey, he decided to take action. He gathered a group of high school students and flew down to start helping in the cleaning and rebuilding process. Katz had no experience in relief and rescue missions. The closest he had gotten was cleaning his house occasionally. But he simply could not ignore the situation.

Even though the professional organizations on-site such as FEMA and the Red Cross seemed to have enormous resources to address the devastating damage, he felt that the little resources he could bring to New Orleans were still important. Since that first mission in 2005, Katz developed an expertise in relief missions to help people and places in tragedy. He established the OU Relief Missions, a nationwide organization that has mobilized high school students for over one hundred missions to date.[1] Those missions were first on-site in Houston, Puerto Rico, New Jersey, Rwanda, and Romania (for Ukrainian refugees), to name a few. His missions include returning to New Orleans every year to continue rebuilding efforts.

If you would ask Ethan Katz if he was thinking about his first mission as an act of courage, he would dismiss it with a simple no. It just needed to be done. The situation presented itself and he decided to take action. What emerged was an act of courage that completely rerouted Ethan Katz's life story. He became an expert in relief missions, collaborating with some of those organizations he once saw as the experts. He shares his knowledge and expertise in mobilizing high school students and transforming their lives through the work of giving and helping others.

Would you consider yourself courageous?

Most courageous people do not. Like Ethan Katz, they simply did what was needed at that moment. The authoring of their life story uncovers the courageous nature of their actions.

Authoring your life is an act of courage. Why? Because you take a set of circumstances created for you prior to your arrival on the scene, combine them with an unknown future, and then decide to act. The action you take is conditional upon many factors you do not control, and yet you find it within you to leap. It is an act of courage because most people get paralyzed by the high degree of helplessness infused into the situation. These people will take no action and opt to remain in a passive mode, waiting for events to happen to them. They dare not take action into their hands.

Authoring your life is an act of taking ownership of your life, even when you do not control all the conditions.

Ben Dean, PhD, of the University of Pennsylvania describes two definitions of courage: Being fearless or having persistence despite hardship or danger. But being fearless is not really the same as having courage. If one does not have fears, then there is nothing to conquer. Instead, the existence of fear allows courage to emerge.

Dr. Dean lists a variety of fears that drive results when demonstrating courage:

- Fear of job loss

- Fear of poverty

- Fear of losing friends

- Fear of criticism

- Fear of ostracism

- Fear of embarrassment

- Fear of missing out

- Fear of making enemies

- Fear of being perceived as weak

- Fear of losing status

Dr. Dean argues that courage is the response to our deep fears.[2]

As Mark Twain observed, "Courage is resilience to fear, mastery of fear, not absence of fear."[3]

I was once told that fear stands for Fake Emotion Appears Real, an interesting abbreviation that might help you cope with fear.

We take action in spite of our fears in order to reduce their negative impact on us.

## Discovering Our Fears through Authoring Our Life

If we honestly face the aforementioned fears and recognize some of them in our own life, we can discover the biases that are driving our authoring process. They are the negative listening lenses that force our stories into the victimhood zone. Fear is authoring our story as a default when we don't take deliberate effort to author it ourselves.

Fear has maybe paralyzed us in the past. But eventually, an act of courage can address and calm the threat. Recognizing fear is part of the authoring process. It is recognizing our humanity and giving more power to the actual actions we take in spite of fear. The more we uncover our fears, the more aware we are of their existence and their impact on our lives, and the more we can hone our courage to address them. The act of writing our own chapters brings clarity and understanding that can shape our courage and enhance it.

To discover your fears and overcome them, start with the following questions:

- How do you define courage?

- Who represents courage in your eyes? Why?

- What fears did they have to overcome to conduct the act of courage? (You know everyone has fears, right?)

- What motivated them to overcome the fear?

- If you considered yourself courageous, what act would define your courage? (If you can't find a big one, start small.)

- What was the fear you had to overcome?

- How did you do it? Did you overthink it or rip off the bandage?

We all approach overcoming fear differently. Some will just jump in. Others will have to read about and rationalize it until they are convinced to try and be courageous. Some need simulations to practice showing courage (think people who fear flying and go to special simulation sessions). But the ultimate motivation to overcome fear is observing someone's impact on others (impressing them is a form of impact, too). We get out of our comfort zone of fear and predictability when we are called to be courageous for someone else.

When you ask someone if they were courageous during a certain act, the most common answer is no. They simply did what had to be done at that moment. It was the most natural reaction to the situation at hand. While they may have been aware of the existence of fear, it didn't prevent them from taking action. Others who didn't take action were paralyzed by their fear, and that fear resulted in no action—which is still a form of action.

## Fear as an Accelerator to a Courageous Life

Fear isn't the worst thing in the world. In fact, we might owe a debt of gratitude to our fear.

Would we have dared to achieve those ambitious goals without fear's existence?

Would we experience the thrill of success to the same degree without the fear that drove these actions?

No. Without fear, we would not have risen to the version of ourselves we are today. We would not have reached our heights of performance without the fear that drove us. The fear of poverty drove us to achieve financial stability and security. The fear of disappointing others creates a kinder version of us that is more engaging with the world. The fear of embarrassment leads us to get out there and be more resilient to others' comments.

Make no mistake, fear may drive us to extremely stupid and dangerous acts. The fear of poverty may drive us to steal and cheat, as some people have done. The fear of disappointing others may lead to constant people-pleasing that may result in losing ourselves. Those are chapters that people chose to author because of their fears. Choosing to conquer fear (or its negative alternative) validates the power of fear to shape the story of our lives and act as catalysts in the evolving narrative.

Being courageous is not a declaration; it is action. Authoring our life is the ultimate form of courage, because it is acting in unknown and uncontrolled conditions and creating beautiful outcomes. Fear plays a role in the courage we choose to demonstrate. It is not just the negative side of courage. It is, with more understanding and clarity, the accelerator of courage.

*What will drive you to activate your courage?*

## CHAPTER 11

# The Authored Story, Free of Influencers

I don't know how she snuck into my feed. I could never figure out those algorithms.

But every day, she posts a video of herself selecting her clothing, shoes, and bag for the day. She shares this with me and the tens of thousands of her followers who in return provide her with their validating comments and emojis, as well as some nasty comments about her figure and choice of clothing.

I still cannot fully understand the appeal of this process. For her, I guess she feels as if she is famous, or maybe the validation supports her self-confidence. Maybe she thinks she helps people. For her followers, is it voyeurism? A form of social support, or a way to seek fashion advice (which I can't fully understand because every person is very different in body shape, style, skin color, etc.)?

Welcome to the influencer economy.

What started as sharing with friends and family has become a huge enterprise for selling products, selling advice, and influencing people's decisions and choices. According to research, we now prefer influencers' viewpoints over formal information from companies and brands. Sixty-three percent of consumers will consult influencers before making a purchase. Our lives and preferences have become a reflection of the choices of people we don't really know, and we take slivers of their life stories and try to imitate them.

Influencers come in different flavors and sizes as well. There are mega-influencers with millions of followers and micro-influencers with fewer than one hundred thousand followers. They focus on different areas of life, from self-care to beauty to fashion, home décor, cars, and travel. You are likely to follow several influencers to cover all your interests.

Most of all, they have opinions. They like to tell you what is good or bad. It's not journalism. It is sharing personal opinions. The increasing power of influencers has made them the new darlings of brands paying them to promote their new products. The marketing field is undergoing a transformation, with agencies dedicated to developing and representing these new "talents" and marketing their services to brands seeking to reach their customers.

For many, the influencers are the new journalism. Entertaining delivery of facts and knowledge in a concise format suits the new generation of readers and viewers.

The reality is far from it. Let's examine the challenges with this new form of content creation and distribution:

- **The distorted picture of perfection**—Social media posts and videos tend to reflect only perfect pictures of life stories. Those who post work hard to convey perfection in a way that creates a distorted picture of life. Those quick snippets of faux perfection are not life, but they create an illusion that leaves everyone else frustrated, anxious, and unfulfilled when they can't achieve it.

- **Authenticity, yet not**—Those slivers of stories are not the full narrative of those influencers. They choose to tell a partial story, so it's not an authentic one. This again deceives their followers with false belief and a wrong comparison.

- **Economic agenda**—Many influencers are motivated by a financial agenda. Their fame is translated into financial gains. While we think we receive authentic, next-door-neighbor advice, we really are exposed to commercial content in its worst version: disguised as honesty.

- **Self-appointed**—Many influencers are simply self-appointed. Their expertise is not formal or complete in any way; they simply decided that they are qualified. The validation they get from their followers magnifies this self-aggrandizement.

- **Addiction to attention**—The addiction to attention, likes, and comments makes influencers do whatever it takes for another like and comment. On a flight to Newark, I was sitting next to a famous lifestyle influencer who carefully documented every step of the flight (including the food) and shared it with all her followers. When we landed, she picked up her luggage arranged in a certain way and again filmed the special occasion for all her thirsty followers who desperately needed to see how the luggage made the flight. What's the purpose of all of that? What do followers get from this exposure?

- **Getting too extreme**—Internet challenges, anyone? How risky and stupid they have become. It came to a point that the social media companies needed to monitor them and remove some.

Influencers pretend to be the next sages of the new flock. Instead, an ego-driven, like-addicted culture is evolving that makes people not only fail to be themselves but also pitch to others an extreme, perfect life that doesn't exist. The impact on teens is evident through many studies such as one labeled "fear of missing out" (FOMO), which illustrates that anxiety, depression, and the need to be physically touched are related to problematic smartphone use. Problematic smartphone use is defining who you are through the social activities you conduct on your smartphone, which are beyond your control. The sense of FOMO combined with feelings of inadequacy, isolation, and dissatisfaction with one's life story cause serious damage to one's ability to develop their own story.[1] Social media influencers are simply seeking and benchmarking their life according to a fake version of an extreme narrative, all produced to solicit money under the disguise of authenticity.

Nothing can be more devastating and damaging to one's development. The average person spent 151 minutes on social media a day in 2023, compared to only 90 minutes ten years earlier. If you add this to the distortion of content, the frequency of exposure means that we need to actively work on removing its influence from our feed to allow ourselves to focus on who we are and our real story.

Focusing on authoring your life story is more critical than ever. You need to work on staying in your own focus and not getting distracted by the fake stories populated and marketed by others. Ask yourself the following questions:

- Which influencers do you follow most?

- What are their key messages?

- What qualifies them to speak on their key issues?

- What do you get from following them?

- How have they influenced your choices?

- How do they make you feel?

- Do they try to sell products or services?

- Who would you be if you never met those people?

- How would you characterize your relationship with them?

- How would you spend your time if you were not following them?

- How would your decisions change if you were not following them?

While my tone of voice and choice of words may expose a certain bias against influencers, the scope of my argument is not about the phenomenon. I am merely focusing on the need to proactively author your life story and be focused on it consciously. If you don't, influencers pose the risk of leading you to write an unfinished story. With influencers, the risk of ending up with a false story that is not ours is magnified tenfold. The need to author proactively and define who we are (and what we learn in the process) becomes critical under a high-frequency assault of fake picture-perfect stories, all from influencers who stand to make money off of convincing you that there is one way to do everything—their way.

Today, more than ever, you need to own your accurate story and let it authentically develop based on who you are and your life experiences. Keep it honest, personal, and uninfluenced by strangers.

*What influences do you need to remove*
*to develop your authentic story?*

# PART 2

# Author How?

## CHAPTER 12

# Let's Write a Chapter

OVID-19 is a chapter in everyone's life story. Some suffered more than others, but no one in the world escaped the pandemic. Whether people experienced changes to work conditions, home isolation, or, even worse, knew people who had or died from the virus, we all lived through it. But did we take the time to incorporate it into our life story? What is the role of this experience in our overall journey? What did we take from it to live better moving forward?

It is easier to write a chapter about a dream that turned into an achievement. From the beginning, you were the hero of the story and could easily identify the efforts you took to fulfill the dream. The reason is simple: you felt in control throughout the whole process. You initiated the dream, put forth the effort, chose to make the sacrifices, and hopefully you successfully achieved the goal.

But what happens when life happens unexpectedly? In the famous words of Allen Saunders, life is what happens when you're making other plans. No one planned for COVID-19. No one expected the massive disruption to the world because of it. The starting point of this story is victimhood. We all started as victims.

In fact, when we examine the COVID-19 impact, we realize that humanity suffered a major disruption to an underlying belief. Previously, we believed that we were in the good hands of experts and authorities. The promise of the authorities is that they will handle tasks or situations where we do not possess the expertise or resources. For example, doctors will help with our health, police will enforce law and order, and artists will make the world a more beautiful place. We subconsciously counted on medical authorities, legal authorities, academic authorities, religious authorities, and authority in general to guide us in the land of the unknown and unexpected.

Then came COVID-19, and all those in charge responded with the same exact message: "I don't know." None of our traditional authorities were ready for the pandemic. They were helpless and looking for answers. As a result, humanity as a whole and individuals suffered extreme helplessness. We lost the foundation of our life in the form of trust in experts who were supposed to guide us. It wasn't only the physical restrictions and the removal of loved ones that led to this state of victimhood, but more so the mental loss of authority figures that left us feeling exposed.

Although we saw significant growth in drug and alcohol consumption during this time, we also witnessed something else. Early on, we saw five-star hotels opening their doors free of charge to the unhoused. We saw restaurants giving away food.

We saw volunteers helping the elderly everywhere. We witnessed companies joining forces to find solutions and invent medicines. We saw humanity in some of its most beautiful states: helping each other and caring.

Was the COVID-19 pandemic a story of victimhood or of heroism? I'd argue that it was a story of choice, one that individuals, families, organizations, and societies made to elevate above the victimhood (or not). Victimhood was a catalyst to rise to the better version of ourselves and discover, in some cases, resilience and creativity we didn't know existed within us. We chose not to be victims, even in the shadow of a global phenomenon that rendered every one of us helpless and incapable of solving the whole problem. We could choose to focus on the power we did have, converting our helplessness into empowerment. When the opportunity presented itself, we discovered the skills that allowed us to make an impact.

## What Is Your COVID-19 Chapter?

Imagine you sit down with your grandchildren who have only ever read about COVID-19. What would you tell them? What is the story you share? Let's develop that story together.

**Section 1: The unexpected is emerging**—Many of us saw what was happening as a remote story, something evolving elsewhere. It took us some time (months, really) to realize that a pandemic was coming that would impact us and our communities, friends, and families. Even as it did come closer, "it will not happen to me" affected many (as evidenced by resistance to suggested measures like washing hands and wearing masks).

- As you heard about COVID-19 starting to spread from China to the world in early January 2020, where were you?

- What did you think about the threat?

- What was your initial reaction?

- Did you take any action?

**Section 2: It's hitting home**—You then heard about a person you know who was in a hospital or even died from the virus. Now it felt like this was no longer a problem far away. It was here. Yet, medical experts had no real way of treating it. No medicine existed and a vaccine was years away. And beyond the medical experts, everyone from the UN and WHO, to the government and academia—all our experts seemed stunned by this pandemic.

- How did you feel at this point?

- As you saw authorities struggle and realized there was no magic cure, how did it affect your confidence?

- What fears or anxieties did you experience?

- How did you cope with the fear and anxiety?

**Section 3: Stuck at home**—For the first time in most of our lives, we heard about government mandates to stay at home. We were required to avoid human contact. Hugs were considered dangerous. Handshakes were risky. We washed our hands constantly—all concepts your grandchildren will struggle to comprehend.

- How did it make you feel?

- Whose hug did you miss most?

- What place were you eager to go but couldn't?

- What methods did you find to connect with loved ones?

- What Netflix shows did you binge on?

- What home redecorating did you do during that time?

**Section 4: Must do something**—You were working via Zoom and couldn't see your colleagues in person. Everyone could miss an event at a moment's notice due to testing positive or needing to help a loved one who got infected. Staying at home was taking a toll and became more painful. You were anxious to act. Passivity is not your cup of tea. Totally Zoomed out, you needed to do something. You needed to feel helpful, useful, anything.

- What toll did this new situation take?

- What did you do?

- Who did you help?

- What fears did you overcome?

- How did you overcome them?

- Did you volunteer somewhere?

**Section 5: Emerging a hero**—Somewhere during the process, you started to refuse to be a victim. You started to discover new capabilities. You decided to take on a new hobby—learning how to cook, mastering a new craft, or learning a new language.

- What did you do?

- What was the moment when you said enough is enough?

- When was the point you decided to stop being a victim?

- What power did you discover?

**Section 6: My special superpower**—As you emerge from the passive nature of a victim and try to act, you discover your superpower. Maybe yours is listening, baking cookies, or playing a guitar on your porch to entertain others.

- What is your superpower?

- How did you feel discovering it?

- How did others respond to it?

- What impact did you have on others when you used your superpower?

- How did you enhance and perfect your superpower?

**Section 7: Lesson and growth**—As your superpower activated and you were no longer a victim, you converted helplessness into empowerment. A passive story became a milestone in your life, a story to tell.

- What did you learn about yourself?

- How would you use these lessons to overcome fears in the future?

- What growth did you experience?

- How did it affect you in the long run?

- Did you make some life-altering decisions?

**Section 8: Validation**—For all of us, crisis is a test of our values. We may claim we are someone, but until this value is tested in real life, it is merely an intention. Only a true test can validate if we are the people of values we claim to be. What values of yours did you live during the pandemic? Which values did you manage to live by? How would you react differently if it happened again tomorrow?

## Yesterday's Lessons, Tomorrow's Empowerment

Turning COVID-19 into one of your life's chapters is empowerment for the future. Rising from victims of the unknown to heroes of the present (using our unique superpower) is a story we need to write, learn, and repeat. The more we do so on our life journey, the better and faster we'll emerge from a place of victimhood to heroism.

*How proud would you be of the story
you told your children?*

*What lessons would you share
with your grandchildren?*

## CHAPTER 13

# Deliberate Authoring and Creating New Realities

When our son went off for two months of sleepaway camp, my wife and I decided to do something different. Tired of the classic hotel experience, we approached this vacation differently and wanted to do something immersive. We decided to rent an apartment for a month in Paris and live like locals. On top of that, we added an intensive course in French. Three days a week, we attended an Alliance Française course of three hours each day plus homework.

This was a chapter in our life story we deliberately planned for. It didn't happen to us—we created it. Boy, did we not realize what we had gotten ourselves into (at least me; my wife is more proficient in French).

While the art of authoring your life is about documenting, reflecting, distilling life lessons, and celebrating them, this doesn't only include unexpected life events and serendipitous occurrences. Sometimes authoring can be deliberate and intentional. You can create your own interventions to enrich your life and come out a better or different person because of this deliberate experience.

In preparation for the intensive course, I took Duolingo lessons. Those wonderful three-minute lessons created a sense of confidence in me, and I felt mastering French was going to be a piece of *gateau*.

Reality hit hard the first day of school. I was totally lost. I could not follow the teacher and had no idea what was going on. All the other students seemed to understand and follow, while I was helplessly torn between thoughts of *What was I thinking?* and *What is the teacher saying?* I do not remember the last time I was so clueless and helpless. The class was dark and humbling at levels I hadn't experienced in decades.

As a speaker and executive, I know how to command the room and lead the conversation. You practice how to listen to others. But you never get an experience of not even understanding what is being said to you. It felt like a reset on life. If words were my air, I could hardly breathe. That was a scary feeling.

After two classes where I was completely clueless, I did what I should have done: I asked for the pace to be slower and moved to a lower-level class. The teaching was the same but a bit less intense. Still not much air in the form of words to speak, but I was starting to breathe by having some basic conversation. We are so accustomed to words being our connection, our communication, our expressions, our definition. Here, I was muted.

I wasn't alone in this feeling, but somehow it didn't make me feel better. I had to climb out of the darkness and practice a new language, a new air I had to learn how to breathe.

One unexpected aspect of this experience was that I felt the freedom to fail. As a mature, experienced executive, you quickly assume the know-it-all approach and refrain from admitting you don't know certain things. You act as an answer dispenser in an environment that expects you to solve all problems and know all the answers. This kind of environment I found myself in gives you the option to say, "I don't know," opening you up to new learnings and perspectives. As I was learning French, I had to overcome the inclination to know it all and speak even if I didn't know how to say or pronounce certain sentences. But since I was surrounded by other students who all experienced the same hesitation before speaking, it was somewhat more acceptable to make mistakes. We were all making them.

The ability to make mistakes without fear empowered me to see a world of possibilities outside my comfort zone. I think that it created a willingness to explore things I might otherwise have refrained from doing because I was afraid to fail. (Is cooking on my horizon? Time will tell.)

Now, this was not an experience I *had* to go through. It was an experience I chose. I could quit at any time and go back to the pleasing, comforting experience of speaking in English and retain my old self in its American form. But I chose to impose this new opportunity to refresh myself and insert an unexpected new chapter in my life that could lead to new insights and lessons. Humility ended up being the real and first harsh lesson of this experience.

## The Choice for a Radical New Experience

Exposing yourself to a radical new experience by choice, as opposed to being forced into it, is a sign of resilience and maturity. It's also essential to the process of authoring your narrative.

You are shifting from passive documentation and reflection into taking charge of the twists and turns of your story and your life. You chose to enrich and develop your character and make your life story more interesting, purposeful, and impactful through experiences designed to test you.

I have always claimed that a person cannot name their values; they need to live them. One cannot claim to be generous; they should donate their time, ideas, and money to help others. Values are an act, not a statement. You cannot claim to be courageous without leaving your couch.

Do something that gets you out of your comfort zone. It might be that your courage may mean you do something different than me. For you, it may be volunteering in Africa, learning to dance (if you don't know how), or running a marathon, and for me it will be learning a new language. But courage is about reaching outside of the known and comfortable, creating new realities.

Choosing a deliberate new chapter is taking actions on your stated values and making them an integral part of your personality. It is embedding them through experience and action into your identity. After you have gone through them, you have earned the right to claim that they are part of you. You move them from intentions to personal realities.

As you mature though the process of authoring your story, you will be confronted with the questions:

- How do you choose your next chapter?

- What chapter would develop and build you?

- What would you be without authoring this chapter?

- What powers would it instill in you?

- What impact would you be able to make on the world as a result of it?

Only you will know what that chapter should be.

Drawing on my own experience, I'll say that sometimes you need a personal trainer, someone who will get excited with you, cheer you on, and challenge you to go for it. In my French learning experience, it was my wife. She set the bar and stayed consistent to ensure I was not wavering from the plan.

So while the choice is yours, you may want to reach out to your friends and family and gain support for sticking to the choice and living it to its full potential. The unknown is exciting, but it can be scary. Going back to the old comfortable zone is the easy way out. Choose to author and consider getting a personal trainer to help you stay on the course.

*What will be your next deliberate chapter?*

CHAPTER 14

———————

# Managing the Cynical Voices

"It will never work."

"Smarter people tried and failed. Why would you succeed?"

"If you only had the budget! But you don't."

"The current technology will never support it."

"Replacing the technology is a non-starter."

"It is way too risky."

"I tried it, and it didn't work."

"We hardly have the resources to get the basics done."

"Customers will never pay for it."

"We were not born that way; we have a different DNA."

"You can't change people."

"Other people do it better than us."

"The competition is already ahead of us."

"We are understaffed as it is."

"We have the wrong people for this job."

"We don't have the know-how."

"We lack the expertise."

"Learn to accept your limitations."

"It's a distraction from our current success."

"I didn't go to the right school."

"There are much better qualified people than me for that job."

"My boss will never approve it."

"My spouse will hate me for it."

"I will never be caught doing this."

"It is embarrassing."

"I will look ridiculous."

"Not at this stage of my life."

The voice in our head. It is constantly messing with our plans and filling us with fear, uncertainty, and doubt. The voice is the loudest when the idea is more daring and exciting. That is when the voice takes over and bombards our thoughts with cynical arguments geared to stop the new idea from happening.

After years of successes and failures, this voice becomes more active as the list of cynical excuses grows. It reminds us of all the false starts and failed attempts we made before and reminds us that at the end of the day, there is a higher likelihood of failure than of success. It is very crafty in its excuses.

During a strategy meeting at a large credit card company, I kindly asked the VP of compliance to leave the room and not come back. He was stunned. It is not an action I do often. In fact, I have not done that in years. He stared at the CEO, questioning my request. The CEO just nodded, approving my request.

"But why?" he asked me.

I took a deep breath, wondering if I should tell this client the truth. I decided I would.

"You can't stop your cynical comments, and they interrupt the workshop," I replied.

He looked taken aback.

"But cynicism is my way of dealing with tough reality," he argued.

"Cynicism is not a working tool," I explained. "It is a tool of destruction. No entrepreneur ever claimed to build an amazing organization based on cynicism."

He left the room, frustrated but still not understanding.

This VP, like many other executives, developed a cynical approach to life after years of working on projects that didn't materialize or plans that failed to execute. Cynicism became his way to respond to new ideas. Cynicism amounts to a simple message: "Why bother?"

Cynics destroy the best ideas before even giving them a chance to be considered.

Cynicism often comes across as a funny joke. It's a way to release stress. But like other addictions, it is a vehicle with short-term relief and long-term damaging consequences. Cynicism kills new initiatives and keeps organizations in the comfort zone of mediocrity, operating on autopilot. New ideas and new opportunities are destined to die quickly in toxic environments like the one I experienced at the credit card company.

## Cynicism as the Antigrowth Virus

In working with hundreds of companies around the world on their transformation projects, the first question I ask is, "What are the cynical voices here at the organization?" You cannot implement a new idea or pioneer a new concept when that virus is resisting it with all its might.

The same is true for each and every one of us. Throughout the years, we have experienced failures and plans that did not go as projected. Those experiences became cynical voices that limit our desire to grow and develop. The cynical voices raise a huge red flag with the words, "Why bother?" The bigger and more frightening the idea is, the louder the cynical voices scream, "Stop! Don't do it." The cynical voices become fiercer in our heads in the presence of bold new ideas.

In a corporate setting, people do not often express their cynical doubts but instead search for more politically correct ways to express their fears. But on a personal level, the inner voice has no political correctness. It shoots its cynical arrows straight at the heart of the new idea, attempting to kill it as quickly as possible.

Let's be honest with ourselves as we answer the following questions:

- When was the last time you heard a cynical comment?

- How often do you hear such comments in team meetings or corporate events?

- Do you find these comments funny?

- Do you share cynical jokes about new ideas or people?

- Are cynical comments repeated about one of your colleagues behind their back?

- If a cynical comment were to be made, would you counter it and put the speaker in their place?

- When someone fails at your organization, what are your responses?

- When it comes to your inner voice, what methods do you have to stop cynical comments?

- What ideas did you not pursue in the last year because you were afraid?

- How many of those refused ideas do you regret not pursuing?

- When you gather with friends over beer or wine, is the conversation full of cynical comments and jokes?

- Are you discussing what will work or what will not work?

If you are honest with yourself, you may find you are either a passive or active cynic. It is an easy place to escape to. The cynical jokes may sound funny and provide a quick relief (some of your friends may actually think you are funny). But over the years, those cynical comments pile up as we go through negative experiences and disappointments. It seems justified that we developed this cynical attitude. Technically, we earned the right to be cynical. But if you are honest with yourself, you will quickly discover that cynicism is not a right; it is a burden. A big burden. Over time, as you develop more cynicism in your life, you simply surround yourself with a toxic shield that rejects personal and professional development. It makes your life boringly predictable and unexciting.

## Authoring Is the Antidote

Unauthored experiences and failures turn into cynical voices. In the absence of reflection that results with understanding, acceptance, and lessons learned, the negative experience mutates into a persistent cynical voice that constantly shrinks the future's horizons and prevents you from future development. You become a repeater of the "known, predictable, and expected" and lose the excitement and possibilities of the "new and growing," taking the facts that were sometimes not according to your plan and transforming them into a purposeful chapter of your life full of insights.

The cynical voices at organizations are an outcome of the same lack of authoring process. Without transforming the facts into something positive, employees' and executives' experiences mutate into negative voices that will fight the next strategy and instead insist on repeating the "success formula" (also known as the past). Developing an authoring mechanism personally and professionally is a way to stop those negative experiences from mutating into cynicism. Instead, you can channel the voices into relevant knowledge that can be used to assess new ideas and improve them for future development.

If unauthored negative experiences create an acute "why bother?" attitude due to their mutation into cynicism, the same is true with the opposite phenomena. Positive experiences and success can easily mutate into overconfidence and hubris. Every new idea, though not properly evaluated for viability, will be pursued in the name of our invincible character. When, due to a lack of authoring, guidelines are not instituted to assess new ideas and opportunities, every one will be pursued—which can be reckless and irresponsible. If cynicism attempts to stop the pursuit of new ideas, hubris can create the opposite effect. While cynicism may strip us of future development and growth, hubris will send us into multiple reckless pursuits that can cause damage as well.

Authoring is stopping events and experiences from mutating into an uncontrolled emotional reaction. Instead, it provides a balanced understanding of events and leads toward utilizing them for the better pursuit of future opportunities. It makes us smarter, both in being open to new ideas and cautious based on our past experience.

*What cynical comment should you get rid of?*

---

## CHAPTER 15

# The Defining Milestones
# of Your Journey

"What is the one defining moment you can point to that turns a normal child into an at-risk one?"

I presented this tough question to a CEO of a national organization treating teenagers at risk ranging from experiences of violence to sexual and drug abuse.

He had to think about it.

"There are many reasons," he said. "Each case is unique."

"But if you try to distill all those reasons into one root cause, what would that be?" I pressed.

He paused for a while and finally said, "If I have to come up with one main reason, then it is the moment that someone in their childhood said something cynical to them and broke their innocence."

The answer shocked me. I think it actually shocked him too.

"Just one cynical comment can do that?" I asked.

"Yes," he said with confidence.

Imagine the power we all have with the words we use.

It is incomprehensible that one cynical comment can destroy lives, yet that's what it does to thousands of children. I doubt the adults who say these cynical comments even remember saying them. They likely uttered a comment in a moment of distress or frustration. But for that child, it was a defining moment. Children are too young to understand the shades of emotional responses of adults. They view the world in a holistic black and white lens. Adults know everything. They are the authorities. If they say it, it must be true. If the adult is a close relative they learn to lean on and trust, that's an even greater authority.

While our lives are full of moments of happiness, sadness, excitement, disappointment, and anticipation, not all those moments are defining. Defining moments are special, as their experience illuminates and amplifies milestones on our journey and may change the trajectory of our path. They are moments that meant we had to make a certain choice or left us with a life lesson that will stay with us forever. While many sad or happy moments will come and go, by and large they will be forgotten and replaced with similarly sad or happy moments. Defining moments, on the other hand, are here to stay. They are there to shape our lives and give us the path and purpose that is uniquely ours. Defining moments are the clear milestones that make our journey distinctively ours.

## Distinctively You, Courtesy of the Defining Moments

As we author our life's chapters, it's important to recognize the defining moments. There are two types of defining moments:

conscious defining moments and subconscious defining moments. The conscious defining moments are deliberate and known to us up front. These include events such as selecting a job or deciding to marry someone. They are big commitments led by a leap of faith and the promise of a different life. The day after making such a decision is destined to be hopefully richer, adding new experiences and colors to our life. Knowing these defining moments allows us to stay in control and ensures they define us in a positive way.

The subconscious defining moments are quite different and result in behavior we often do not control. Like the aforementioned cynical comments, events and statements in our childhood can steer our life in a certain direction, but only in retrospect are we aware of its influence. Consider these questions:

- Do you find yourself pleasing people at the expense of your own wishes?

- Do you believe that you are not allowed to show emotions because they will make you seem weak and vulnerable (and society does not like vulnerable people)?

- Are you focusing on being liked by as many people as possible at the expense of living your unique self?

- Do you wear clothing that you like or that others like?

- Do you watch for approval?

- Do you find yourself reflecting on what others are saying more than stating your own opinion?

- Do you hesitate to share your voice because you are afraid of being rejected?

- Do you wait for others to share their opinion first?

- Do you join your friends in activities they like more than they join in on ones you like?

- Do you feel a responsibility to be a good child for your parents?

Any of these behaviors indicate that you are trying to compensate for something. They are common among people who suffered some kind of childhood trauma.

Was the trauma a nasty comment by a childhood friend? A bullying experience? A boycott in school? A sibling who was favored over you, or a parent who set extreme standards? It may have been a simple statement said once that nevertheless created a compensating behavior in you that attempted to refute the statement but instead twisted you into someone else. It was a defining moment.

A subconscious defining moment is more than a contributing moment like happiness, achievement, or failure. It is a moment that shapes your future behavior and changes the direction of your trajectory. Your parents, family members, or childhood friends may never intend to shape your trajectory that way. They probably do not remember the time and place when they said the defining statement. But you do. It resides in your subconscious until, when triggered, it resurfaces to impact your conscious state. You relive that moment as it feeds into the compensating behavior, again and again.

It is imperative that as we author our life's story, we take special note of the defining moments. We need to evaluate them and ensure that we are happy with the way they shape our lives and make them uniquely us. After all, authoring our lives is not a documentation process that accepts everything as is. The real power of authoring our lives is the drive to act from past experiences, creating a better future and a better self.

As we find ourselves in behaviors that seem to contradict what we want and may subject us to others' wishes, we need to explore the subconscious defining moments that led us to these behaviors. We all relive those moments, but we may not link our destructive behaviors to them. Linking and accepting that these are defining moments will help us rationalize what is seemingly an impulsive, uncontrollable behavior. We can take charge of our future and infuse it with more deliberate behavior while shedding the uncontrollable attitudes we hate so much.

Our life is full of moments, but not all moments are created equal. Some moments charge our life with emotions. Other moments are the defining ones that create noticeable milestones in our life journey. Recognizing them and taking control of their outcome will enable us to author an ever-better story of our life and move from documenting to improving our future life journey.

*What childhood experience do you relive often?*
*How did it define your life?*

## CHAPTER 16

# Words Create Realities

As many personality tests indicate, we engage in life in diverse ways. Take the DiSC personality test, for example. The test results describe people in one of four profiles: dominance, influence, steadiness, and conscientiousness.[1] As the personalities' descriptive words indicate, different people approach life differently. While dominance may represent a results-oriented person, consciousness represents an analytical person who is concise and deliberate. This is quite different from the enthusiasm-driven person.

I once collaborated with a client who required all their employees to place their personality test results on their desks, so they were visible. This was meant to help people determine the communication and engagement style of different employees and encourage engaging with them on their terms.

While it might be difficult to memorize specific personal traits and adapt your style to each person, there is a way to determine your engagement style: the words you choose to use.

As you author the story you call your life and document your experiences, it is important to note your choice of words in the process. Different words can express the same situation, but they may lead to vastly different narratives.

Witnessing a national demonstration, I noticed that many of the protesters chose terms like "traitor" to describe their opponents. Such word choice resulted in what I would call "shutdown terminology." But with a word like "traitor," we portray the opponent not as a person with a distinct set of values and opinions but as a personality not worthy of a mutual dialogue. We see beyond the opinions and categorize the person themselves as unworthy of a discussion. That choice of word is meant to shut down the conversation and not allow for any engagement.

The words we choose to describe our life and author its narrative are similarly loaded. Certain word choices will turn the story into an inspirational one, while others will be devoid of any emotion and leave us with a flat, unengaging narrative. Some words will focus solely on the outcome (success or failure), while others will describe the learning process during the journey and respect it as part of the overall story.

Let's examine your choice of words. The outcome may surprise you, as the choice is not conscious. The words that come to mind from the subconscious are the true descriptors of the story as it resides in your experience. They therefore shape the power of that experience and your attitude toward it. Being more conscious of your choice of words can adapt and tweak the narrative, shifting it from one emotional state to another.

## Discover Your Choice of Words

Write down a description of a recent meeting you had with someone. Try to write without thinking too much about it, simply describing the interaction. After writing this short (or long) paragraph, review it and identify the theme of your description. Some questions to help you identify the theme include:

- Is your description factual or emotional?

- Did you describe the journey in detail or rush to the bottom line?

- Are you portrayed as an active or passive participant?

- Did you enjoy the interaction?

- Did it provide you with a sense of accomplishment?

These questions will allow you to identify the theme of your description. Do not change it as you review these questions. The idea is for you to understand the baseline of your choice of words. When you identify the theme of your description or story, you can now move to the next step: identify the words. What words or groups of words appear most often?

Some typical categories of word choices that lead to your story development follow:

- **Results oriented**—Words that sum up the outcome and ignore the process and the pain/emotions associated with the experience. Words such as *results*, *outcome*, *bottom-line achievement*, and *failure* will star in your description.

- **Respect for the journey**—You are placing emphasis on the journey and the process and less on the outcome. Words such as *the next steps*, *process*, *journey*, and *milestones* will be evident in your description.

- **Every detail matters**—Your description is detail-oriented to a point that the trees are beautifully described . . . but where is the forest? Colors, images, and intricate details will be woven into your descriptions.

- **Emotions above all**—Life is about feeling it, and your choice of words are emotional by nature. Facts matter less and emotions reign supreme. Words such as *felt*, *devastated*, *frustrated*, and *love* will be leading your narrative.

- **Inspirationally motivational**—Your words are inspirational. You wear specific lenses that turn every lemon into lemonade. Words such as *hope*, *aspiration*, *empowerment*, and *possibilities* will be staples in your story.

- **Compassionate and forgiving**—Your words are full of compassion. They recognize that no gain comes without pain and focus on forgiving and love-giving. Words such as *forgiving*, *understanding*, and *respecting* will be integral to the way you craft the story.

- **Demanding and uncompromising**—You may sound like a drill sergeant. Great achievements come from setting ambitious standards and pursuing them ruthlessly. Words such as *standards*, *achievement*, *excellence*, and *exceeding expectations* will be key to your narration.

- **Accurately painful**—While you may have achieved a great deal, your focus is on the pain experienced on the way to the gain. You depict it with the full spectrum of suffering you have experienced. Words such as *pain*, *price to pay*, *loss*, and *failure* will be featured in the narrative.

- **Celebratory and exciting**—It is the party that meets you at the finish line. You are celebrating and excited. Words such as *congratulations*, *excitement*, *awesome*, and *magical* will find themselves in the core of your narrative.

As you can see, the choice of words (although not intentional and mostly intuitive) will paint your story development in a distinct way. The same story can be told in different ways, where the words function as the key to its development. The emphasis will be given to one aspect of the story, such as the pain of the journey or the celebration of success, and will downplay other aspects of the story. In reality, all aspects are important to fully evaluate the story and commit it as a lesson-driving chapter in your life story. Being conscious of your approach will enable you to make sure that your authored chapters are more well-rounded and not all written the same way.

## The Distillation of Words over Time

How do we choose our words? It is a long, ongoing process. While we may want to believe that it is a conscious process that starts with understanding context, audience, tone, and where we want to apply our message, there is more to it. Throughout the years, we are influenced by our parents and teachers, and how other people we admire describe situations and stories. We are influenced by their choice of words and develop a language that reflects those choices.

If our mother was playing the blame game and told her stories as a series of cases of victimhood where she was a passive player in the world of dominant people, then there is a likelihood that we will assume a similar lens in life and author our lives as a story of victimhood. We will see the pain and suffering caused to us but will find no ownership or inspiration in what we do and the future we have. If one of our professors in college was a staunch believer in entrepreneurship and told stories of individuals who beat all the odds and succeeded despite the difficulties, our perspective may be shared accordingly. We will start describing our narrative as a journey of overcoming obstacles.

Our choice of words was shaped over time.

After reviewing the narrative you wrote and identifying the theme and words category, would you say you are happy with your word choice? Is it going to help you author a story you will be proud of? If not, change your choice of words and then your story will start moving in the direction you wish it to. The default choice is the one dictated by your past. Changing it will require full awareness and daily practice.

Choosing words does not mean you ought to be all motivation and inspiration. Like personality tests, we have distinctive styles and approaches. Some people enjoy deliberate reflection, while others thrive on inspirational and motivational words. Some people gain strength from touching the pain before recovering, while others see beauty in the milestones of the journey. Be yourself. In your choice of words, make sure you are being deliberate and authentic to your own style and avoid defaulting to the retelling of someone else's story.

*What is one word that describes you the best?*

CHAPTER 17

# Controlling the Unknown

When you face the unknown, how do you feel? For some, the lack of control leads directly to fear. For others, the unknown is exciting, full of unexpected surprises. They seek excitement, and the unknown provides it. It can also depend on the context. If the unknown is forced on us unexpectedly, such as a medical surgery, you may experience more fear than excitement. If the unknown is bungee jumping off the Sydney bridge, you may feel more excitement than fear.

Both unknowns generate extreme emotions for a remarkably simple reason: We lack control of what's coming next. We are blind to the actual experience even if we prepare ourselves by reading about it or watching a YouTube video. Reading or watching about such an experience is not the same as actually going through it, nor does it provide us with control over what is going to happen or how we'll feel about it.

Authoring our life's story is a process in which we can regain control. Even during an unexpected, unknown event where we felt completely helpless and out of our comfort zone (by a long shot, sometimes), the authoring process allows us to regain control.

How does it work? When authoring an event, we go through different layers of understanding, acceptance, and learning:

**Stage 1: Understanding**—At the first stage of authoring an experience, we merely process the event and document what happened to us. We relive the images, smells, lights, colors, words, and everything that took place during the event. We review the event from a vantage point of knowing its end, which releases fear and pressure, and we notice details we might have missed during the actual event. We get a full and complete picture of what we experienced.

**Stage 2: Acceptance**—During the acceptance stage, we evaluate our emotions toward the event. Recalling how we felt during the event (fear, excitement, happiness, content, anticipation, disappointment, etc.) adds a flavor to the description created during stage 1 of understanding. It adds your personal perspective and then morphs into how you feel about it now. How would you assess the event now that you know its end and outcome? What do you feel toward the outcome, and how do you feel about your emotions during the event? Many of us scream at a roller coaster ride, and some may cry or even throw up. But most would claim afterward that it was all worth it and want to do it again. Understanding allows you to evaluate your emotions and how you want to emotionally file it in your memory. Without this stage, the event will remain unresolved, tainted only with the initial emotional reactions and lacking closure and true emotional assessment.

**Stage 3: Learning**—After we review the event objectively during stage 1 of understanding and subjectively during stage 2 of acceptance, we are ready to transform it into the controlled event in our authored story. This is when the objective and subjective experience combine into a learned lesson and insight that will make it a chapter to remember. During this stage, ask yourself the following questions:

1. What did I fear the most? What really happened?

2. What was the source of my helplessness during the event?

3. What was my superpower during the event?

4. What is one thing I learned about the situation?

5. What is one thing I learned about myself?

6. If I could go through this event again, what would I prepare myself for?

7. If I could go through this event again, what would I do the same?

8. If I could go through this event again, what would I do differently?

9. When the event is over, what will I do then?

The answers to these questions will transform your experience from an emotional event to an insightful chapter worth including in your story journey. It will become a milestone.

This is the precise process that will transform a frightening unknown with a complete sense of helplessness into an event that you will regain control over and be ready to face again (if needed).

This process of transforming helplessness into helpfulness is not only applicable to unexpected events. Even the adventures you decide to put yourself through are worth examining. They too have preexisting convictions, unexpected surprises, and personal discoveries about yourself and your superpower. Do not skip the transformation process for adventures you choose to experience. Every unknown and uncontrolled event is an opportunity to regain control and learn how to mobilize it in the future.

Authoring our life story is more than just making sense of the life we did not plan. It is mobilizing what seemingly are passive or even helpless events in life into chapters of power, strength, resilience, and motivation to do better in the future.

*When did you feel you lost control lately?*

_____

*What did you learn from that experience?*

_____

CHAPTER 18

# Authoring Someone Else's Story

*Be yourself; everyone else is already taken.*

As social creatures, we naturally live among people close to us, such as friends, family members, colleagues at work, and employees of vendors we interact with. Our social networks expand to people we meet and interact with on social media and even to individuals we read about. Together they all create our social context. Envy is one of those social traits that makes us constantly compare ourselves to others, the people in our social context, wondering why we don't have what they do. Envy is another way to distort your story authoring because it leads you to take a different path. That path is an attempt to write a chapter in our own story that actually belongs in someone else's story.

The damage caused by envy is well documented. It leads people to depression and anxiety, as they are constantly busy comparing themselves with others and feeling themselves lacking in so many ways. That constant comparison focuses our efforts on trying to achieve or possess things others do and has us living in constant stress about why their story doesn't fit ours. It's a pursuit of a moving target because we're already seeking to possess something else even when we achieve or manage to acquire what others have. There are so many people in the world to compare ourselves to that we will be constantly disappointed.

In the context of authoring, envy is a distortion. It aims at goals that are not authentically ours, and it is a story that doesn't reflect you authentically.

## But envy is motivational . . . isn't it?

Some argue that envy is a great accelerator for people's motivation. By seeing other achievements, we aim higher and raise our standards. Their achievements inspire us to rise up and make more of our lives.

On the surface, that argument sounds reasonable . . . until we dig deeper. There is a distinct difference between envying someone's efforts or hard work and envying their possessions or achievement. If you follow athletes' path to success and recognize the difficulties they had to conquer—the hard efforts to practice or the tradeoffs they had to make to dedicate themselves to their goals—then envy can be motivational and inspirational. But if your envy's focus is results and possessions, it is a futile exercise in comparing yourself to other people's stories. Admiring efforts and the power of the human spirit is a great exercise in rising to the highest version of yourself. Coveting possessions and outside validation is not inspirational.

Most people's envy focuses on the end results and not the efforts. In comparing ourselves to others and seeking their success, we fail to see them in their full story. Whatever chapter in their lives that you focus on is isolated from their full story. You want to take a period of their life and experience the same. But that doesn't make any sense. Many other stories in the other person's life have built up to the chapter you consider enviable. Just as you cannot take a chapter from Harry Potter, place it within a Jane Austen book, and expect it to excite you in the same way (or even make sense), someone else's chapter will fail to deliver the expected results in your life. One chapter out of context will not fit within who you are and what you are meant to achieve.

The pursuit of others' successes destroys your story. Envy in most cases—unless focused on human spirit, dedication, courage, and the path to success—is an attempt at writing the wrong chapter within your life story. Redirect your envy to learn lessons, not to strive for others' achievements or possessions.

"Good artists borrow, great artists steal." This statement from Pablo Picasso best describes the process of learning in the art world. Stealing is the art of learning from others but creating your own creation. From the blue period to Cubism, Picasso studied the work of other painters and even "borrowed" some of their work, eventually creating new breakthrough art styles that other painters are borrowing from today.

Later in the twentieth century, Pablo Picasso's statement was a source of inspiration for Steve Jobs, the founder of Apple. While Apple was in the computer business, they wrote a different chapter than Dell, HP, IBM, and others. Apple didn't try to imitate. Despite the success and might of the other computer companies, Apple charted their own path. They wrote their own chapter. They didn't just borrow and make the same boring computer as everyone else. They completely elevated the field to create their own version.

Envy the power of the human spirit and its dedication, commitment, willingness to fail, resilience to difficulties, sacrifices, and pursuit of reaching the highest level of excellence and performance. Those are worthy of envy. But then, create your own story. All other stories are already taken.

*What human traits do you envy?*

*Which ones inspire you the most?*

## CHAPTER 19

# Life Stories as Building Blocks

If you're a museum owner who wishes to increase revenues and attendance, arrange an Impressionist exhibit and watch the crowds line up. Add in a Claude Monet and you are almost certain to see your profits rise. The world seems endlessly fascinated with impressionists like Degas, Picasso, Monet, Pissarro, Gauguin, and Manet, to name a few.

But when the first exhibition of Impressionist art debuted, the response was quite different. On April 15, 1874, an exhibition was organized by an "anonymous society of painters, sculptors, printmakers, etc." in a studio in Paris. Journalist Louis Leroy called the artists "Impressionists" as a derogatory term. It described their form of art as shallow and lacking depth, a mere "impression."[1]

Leroy was not alone in his derisive response to the new movement. In fact, the term accurately depicted the artists' intention to divert from the established art styles and depict their own perspective on life as they saw it. In a sense, they ventured to write their own life story and refused to be confined by others' standards and definitions.

As time wore on, this free-spirited approach to art has been accepted by people all over the world. Something in the nervous, rapid, painful brushstrokes of these artists was more authentic and relatable than those of traditional, manufactured composition. It is the authenticity and not the perfectionism that translated into relatable stories.

By deciding to be free of the establishment's shackles, they chose to write their own stories. Their impressions became meaningful because they were the artists' own interpretations.

When we choose to author our life story, we choose to transform what might seem to be boring and meaningless events into meaningful life lessons. We become determined to live life with purpose.

It is a choice to be deliberate, to dream, and to chart a path toward achieving that dream. It is a choice to identify, develop, and refine our skills. It is a choice to be present, aware, and motivated to make the most of every opportunity, whether planned or by surprise. Everything we do has an impact on others, so we can be conscientious of both the privilege and power in our hands.

Authoring is a choice to reflect on an event and create our own narrative, not to leave us with the impression we had at the time of the experience. It is a choice to transform our life's events and occurrences into defined building blocks to make the next chapter of our lives more powerful, daring, and courageous. We do this by learning what questions we should ask the next time so our actions will be better and more impactful. Our mistakes and failures will be minimized. We can develop a better skill set and stronger resilience to face the next opportunity with greater depth and understanding.

Even if you start authoring your life story from here on out, you will still need to revisit some unwritten events from your past. Authoring your life story may require you to go back and take formal stock of what actually happened to you, then convert those documented events into life chapters in your story. You can't reauthor everything, but there are always going to be events you will need to reauthor for yourself as needed. While the documentation may not be as fresh as the events that took place, it is still a worthy effort to make sense of the events happening to you now and that will happen in the future. They may shed light on the behaviors and responses you take next.

Transforming our life events into story chapters is about creating a strong structure of our life with insightful building blocks. Creating our own narrative gives us control over even the most unexpected events and integrates them in a purposeful way into our life's journey.

Go ahead and integrate your life's events. Transform the unresolved into building blocks that will strengthen your life story moving forward.

*What events in your life remain unclear?*

*How can you transform those events into life chapters and building blocks?*

## CHAPTER 20

# Aging with Time:
# Recalibrating the Story

In 2015, I was sitting in a conference room in a Manhattan skyscraper, negotiating the sale of my company to one of the top consulting firms in the world. It was a great honor that my fifteen years of building a business was being recognized by such a prestigious firm. I was looking forward to the completion of the transaction.

On the personal side, I was emotionally and physically exhausted. The economic disaster of 2008–2009 had taken a major toll on my industry, and many of my competitors had either shrunk or disappeared altogether. I lost 90 percent of all my orders within a single month and needed to rebuild. I remember a moment when one of my employees told me, "I know that if you fire us now, the business will survive better. We can see how you are carrying all of us." I teared up. I appreciated the recognition, but the hardship was enormous with five children at home.

I didn't fire anyone, but everyone did take a pay cut so I could keep the business afloat. One of my employees asked if I needed to cut her salary even more. It brought me to tears. She knew I was sacrificing to help us all. She was too but was willing to do even more.

I did manage to rebuild the company. By 2015, we were listed on the Inc. 5000 list as one of the fastest-growing consulting firms and fastest-growing companies in the US. I felt like this was the right time to sell. I had proven our resilience and our ability to come back from a near-death experience and had rebuilt our client list with blue chip brands and a steady increase of business. This was a real company that had weathered the storm, and now I needed a break. The monthly payroll worries, the never-ending invoice collection concerns, the daily grind of managing a business—it all had taken a toll on me. I needed the acquisition to be completed. Fifteen years was a long time. (Did I mention that patience was not my top skill? Is there an entrepreneur who does possess this?)

All the signs during the negotiations were positive. The potential buyers loved the company and its client base. The synergy was clear, and it was a strategic purchase for them, the best circumstances one can hope for. We left with the clear understanding that we were just working on the details and the deal would be completed within thirty days.

I will spare you any more suspense: it didn't. One of the partners changed his mind and decided to try to rebuild our capabilities in-house. I was shattered. I needed this deal so desperately. I already saw myself after the sale and imagined a different, financially stable life for me and my family. I was so close to fulfilling the dream, but the final verdict was a cruel "No!"

This chapter of my life story I was writing at that moment

was painful and filled with disappointment. I was mostly angry for allowing myself to get carried away with images of post-purchase nirvana. That was the main lesson I learned: It ain't over 'til it's over.

Somehow—and I am not sure how—I mustered strength from my depleted reservoirs and got up. I went back to the grind and continued to grow the company. Three years later, I sold my company at a much higher price to a larger company with better prospects. In many ways, I was grateful to the first prospective buyer for not completing the purchase, as it put me and my company in a better position.

Reflecting again on the first failed acquisition, this chapter in my life story is now very different. The facts are the same, but the meaning and consequences now tell a completely different story with the perspective of time and evolution of the events that came after. Not only was a better outcome waiting for me, but had that first deal gone through, that partner's hesitation may have resulted in a painful integration and working relationship post-acquisition.

"Smart in hindsight" is usually not a good compliment. It refers to wisdom that is obvious with time. It is wisdom that is acquired when more facts and insights unfold and paint a brighter, clearer picture that allows for a proposed different set of actions. But it is too late to activate those actions, as the opportunity itself is gone.

"Smart in hindsight" got a bad reputation, in my opinion. The perspective-driven wisdom has a great deal of value in our life story evolution. While in the moment of an event, despite all the reflections, our chapter will be written in a certain way. When we are a bit more removed, we may find new beauty that we could not see while emotions and pressure were warping our overall experience.

## Calibration to Strengthen the Story

While documenting the story at the moment it happens is useful, revisiting the narrative in 90 days, 180 days, and a year later adds new dimensions of depth and understanding, strengthening the overall outcome. As new insights unfold, you view the outcome with the perspective of time and examine how it impacted your story development. All these additional dimensions may add to the creation of a richer educational experience overall, and to recalibrate your sense of purpose and the role it plays in your life's story.

When recalibrating your life story, consider the following questions:

- In the context of time, how did your story evolve?

- What happened after and as a result of your previous chapter?

- How did your emotions change?

- Did the outcome of the chapter drive you to do something you didn't expect?

- Did the absence of an expected outcome provide space for other actions?

- When exploring the impact on others around you, did this chapter demonstrate a different meaning?

When recalibrating the chapter, you will not change the facts (unless new facts you didn't know at the time of the initial writing emerge afterward), but rather examine them with fresher, wider lenses of time, people, and other events surrounding your story. In this context the chapter emerges stronger, more insightful. Most importantly, you will become wiser and prouder as a result (yes, in hindsight). There is nothing more powerful than reflecting on and discovering that what seemed to have been a failure became a powerful driver for a better life. This is when an event becomes a milestone. Milestones are usually difficult to see while we are in the middle of them. But later, in the context of the journey, a milestone becomes clearer and its contribution to the journey more powerful.

I am a huge fan of Rabbi Jonathan Sacks's writing. I'm sharing this story of his with you as is:

> There is a story I find very moving, about how in 1966 an eleven-year-old African-American boy moved with his family to a hitherto white neighborhood in Washington. Sitting with his brothers and sisters on the front step of the house, he waited to see how they would be greeted. They were not. Passers-by turned to look at them, but no one gave them a smile or even a glance of recognition. All the fearful stories he had heard about how whites treated Blacks seemed to be coming true. Years later, writing about those first days in their new home, he says, "I knew we were not welcome here. I knew we would not be liked here. I knew we would have no friends here. I knew we should not have moved here."

As he was thinking those thoughts, a woman passed by on the other side of the road. She turned to the children and with a broad smile said, "Welcome!" Disappearing into the house, she emerged minutes later with a tray laden with drinks and cream cheese and jam sandwiches which she brought over to the children, making them feel at home. That moment—the young man later wrote—changed his life. It gave him a sense of belonging where there was none before. It made him realize, at a time when race relations in the United States were still fraught, that a Black family could feel at home in a white area and that there could be relationships that were colorblind. Over the years, he learned to admire much about the woman across the street. But it was that first spontaneous act of greeting that became, for him, a definitive memory. It broke down a wall of separation and turned strangers into friends.

The young man, Stephen Carter, eventually became a law professor at Yale and wrote a book about what he learned that day. He called it *Civility*. The name of the woman, he tells us, was Sara Kestenbaum, and she died all too young. He adds that it was no coincidence that she was a religious Jew. "In the Jewish tradition," he notes, such civility is called "*chessed*—the doing of acts of kindness—which is in turn derived from the understanding that human beings are made in the image of God."

"Civility," he continues, "itself may be seen as part of *chessed*: it does indeed require kindnesses toward our fellow citizens, including the ones who are strangers, and even when it is hard."

He adds:

> To this day, I can close my eyes and feel on my tongue the smooth, slick sweetness of the cream cheese and jelly sandwiches that I gobbled on that summer afternoon when I discovered how a single act of genuine and unassuming civility can change a life forever.[1]

Sara Kestenbaum might not have planned to change the world when she spread cream cheese and jelly on those bread slices and served them to a young Mr. Carter. She probably didn't even know the little child's name. She just did the right thing at that moment to convert loneliness into a small moment of welcoming togetherness. She didn't live to see the big impact a simple cream cheese–and-jelly sandwich made.

But we can reflect on our life chapters and examine the greater impact. Hindsight can be a powerful tool to develop future understanding. It's no different than reading history to understand future developments. We should not let those events pass by without a journey context and impact examination. The gift of time doesn't only heal but makes us wiser and often prouder. Our life chapters mature like wine and take on new flavor. Meaningless events become infused with purpose, but only if we reflect, recalibrate, and seek to infuse them with meaning.

While we go through hardships or joyful life events, we ought to give ourselves the gift of strength through purpose. This can be achieved when we convert the present experience into time-perspective life lessons.

*What lessons would you draw*
*from past experiences?*

*How often do you reflect on*
*your previous chapters?*

# PART 3

## Author Now!

CHAPTER 21

# Evolving Your Childhood Stories

At the age of eighteen, Steve Bartlett wrote in his diary that by the age of twenty-eight, he wanted to become a millionaire and own a sporty Aston Martin car. He achieved this goal by the age of twenty-three. The British serial entrepreneur and producer of the *Diary of a CEO* podcast came from a single-parent household where his mother struggled to provide for her children. Those experiences of poverty left a major mark on him and drove him to the goal of becoming rich. As he shared his story on the podcast with Simon Sinek (the author of *Start with Why*), he reflected on this success and declared it in retrospect to be something very different.[1]

Bartlett's true motivation was insecurity. The drive to become rich was not to make a difference in the world; it was merely a way to compensate for childhood pains and difficulties. I was impressed by his insight. It takes courage to reflect on success, understand its true meaning, and be vulnerable.

Growing up is tough for a child. We experience life without a guidebook, struggling to fit in, build friendships, understand fairness and happiness and our ever-evolving identity. Every small event can drive our growth in a different, sharp direction. As I shared in a previous chapter, one cynical comment by an adult can send a child on a path of drug abuse or violence. Parents cannot be there to protect us in every interaction with other children or adults. We navigate alone and without a compass or map. We write the first chapter of our life story often without knowing how to actually write.

In sixth grade, I was invited to the first mixed-gender birthday party of the year. I was naïve and unprepared for what would be my first "tween" rite of passage. I saw my friends dancing together, hugging each other, and some were kissing. I had no idea how to do any of that. I sat on the side and stared, puzzled and uncomfortable.

At home, I shared this experience with my mother. My mother disapproved of such behavior, so she shared it with my teacher to see if she could try and curb the behavior. My teacher in turn told the class that it was too early for them to start dancing and making out. The teacher, in her infinite wisdom, mentioned my mom as the person who brought it to her attention. She thought she was giving my mom positive recognition. I disagreed—and so did the rest of the class. That day, on the way back home, I was attacked by one of my classmates, unhappy about what I'd told my mother. He threw my books and notebooks on the floor and humiliated me in front of the other children.

I remember this event vividly. I remember exactly where I

stood (by the fire department), what I was wearing, what the boy said, how the tears and snot running down my face felt as I walked home—and this memory doesn't leave me. Needless to say, I was never invited to any more class parties. I left the school at the end of that year anyway, but I never forgot that burning experience.

This is a childhood story that defined a path in my life. If I had stayed at that school, I would have probably ended up in a very different place in my life (and possibly would never have written this book).

For some of us, those childhood stories are drivers for certain behaviors, motivations, and goals. But often, they are not healthy drivers and initiate insecure ways for us to compensate for the difficult growing process. An important part of writing our life's story is visiting those stories, touching those scars (that may still be open wounds), and dealing with them with mature thinking to help us convert them from pain to progress.

Pain plus reflection leads to progress. I do not recall where I first heard this insight, but I love it. We all want to feel that we make progress. Those unresolved, unwritten childhood chapters may keep us back or send us in the wrong direction (pursuing insecurities instead of real, meaningful goals). Some of us may prefer not to touch those moments. But the longer we leave them unresolved, the more they will burden us. These chapters were written by children with a limited ability to understand events or transform them into insights. The insights we probably processed out of them were naïve and painful. They deserve a mature makeover. They deserve to be added as mature chapters with insecurities turned into strength through experience.

As you approach your childhood unresolved stories to turn them into mature chapters of your life, consider the following questions:

- What exactly happened at that event?

- Who were the players in the event?

- What was your understanding at the time?

- When reflecting on it, did the people intend to make you feel the way you did?

- How did this event affect your behavior moving forward?

- What fears are reignited?

- How might these fears and the overall experience influence future choices?

- Which one of those choices do you still love?

- What choices would you make differently?

- What meaning do you find in the choices you made?

Just because we made certain choices due to certain feelings at that moment doesn't mean we cannot infuse them with new purpose and meaning. By infusing them with new meaning, we will not regret the choices we made at that time. In fact, we may be able to elevate the childhood pains and insecurities into solid chapters that helped build a resilient life story.

Don't ignore your childhood stories. They are building blocks in the total life story. They have been written as a draft by a child with limited writing and emotional skills. It is time an adult edits that chapter and elevates it to its rightful place in your life story.

*What childhood story defined your adulthood?*

*How would that story be adapted through your adult eyes?*

## CHAPTER 22

# Owning Your Story: When the Fingers Point in the Right Direction

"Is antisemitism inherent to human character?" I asked Jonathan Rosenblatt, the CEO of the Anti-Defamation League.

The organization he leads has been fighting racial and religious biases and hatred for decades. It started with fighting antisemitism and expanded to raise awareness of hatred of people of all types of national, racial, and religious identities.

He replied, "People's tendency to blame others is inherent to people's psychology."

Antisemitism is a phenomenon that seems to pop up in societies that utilize both capitalism and socialism. People found the Jewish people a scapegoat to everything, from the Black Death to 9/11. You don't even need Jews around to encounter hatred. Jews were expelled from England two hundred years before Shakespeare wrote *The Merchant of Venice*, depicting Jews as misers and greedy. There are fewer than one thousand Jews in Japan as of 2001 (most are expats). Yet *The Protocols of the Elders of Zion* (a widely distributed antisemitic publication worldwide) has influenced literature sold in Japan to this day.[1]

"Blaming," in its essence, is the art of removing any ownership of a situation. We do so sometimes as nations, but often as individuals. We find a scapegoat to blame for whatever good didn't happen to us or any bad things that entered our lives. From friends to parents to teachers to strangers, we may see others creating realities in our lives outside of our control.

The act of blaming others for our personal misfortune is a common human tendency. When faced with challenges or setbacks, some people find it easier to shift responsibility onto external factors rather than accepting accountability for their actions. While it may provide a temporary sense of relief, blaming others can have profound and damaging consequences on an individual's mental, emotional, and social well-being. It can lead to feelings of helplessness, frustration, and a lack of control over one's life.

In his *Harvard Business Review* article titled "Blame Culture Is Toxic. Here's How to Stop It," Michael Timms discusses blame as being more lethal in a relationship than criticism, contempt, defensiveness, and stonewalling.[2] Timms outlines the challenge of people not recognizing that they blame more often than they think. The result is a negative impact on relationships and team dynamics. The inability to take ownership of an issue results in an environment where self-awareness is lacking. Therefore, the ability to correct course and evolve from a bad situation is nonexistent. Timms notes that people tend to not notice how often they blame others. This lack of awareness probably accelerates the negative impact of blame. I once had a CEO who appointed me to a role with the following statement: "Every time I look for someone to blame for a problem, I find out that the finger is pointing at me." He gave me the role simply in order to blame me for his mistakes. While I appreciated his candor and self-awareness, his lack of willingness to own his mistakes was far less admirable. Needless to say, I left the role and the company.

## Effects on Relationships

Blaming others can erode trust and strain interpersonal relationships. When individuals refuse to acknowledge their role in a problem and instead blame others, it creates a toxic dynamic of defensiveness and resentment. The impact of blame on relationships was described in a *Psychology Today* article by Neil Farber, MD. The author lists various negative impacts of blame in a relationship and considers it a form of emotional abuse. Poor self-esteem and reduced intimacy are among the damages resulting from a blame-oriented relationship.[3]

Several factors contribute to the prevalence of blame culture. Media outlets may sensationalize victim stories, emphasizing external factors rather than personal responsibility. This can shape public attitudes, reinforcing the belief that blaming others is a justified response to misfortune. Additionally, societal norms and expectations can play a role, as individuals may not admit fault to avoid shame or social consequences.

In his article "Blame Is Contagious, Except When People Have High Self-Worth," Robert Sutton, author of *The No Asshole*

*Rule*, cites an interesting reason for blame culture. According to research by Nathaniel Fast at USC and Stanford Business School professor Larissa Tiedens, blame is not only the outcome of low self-esteem and a fear of the consequences of your mistake, but it is apparently contagious.[4] Seeing someone blaming others gives us permission to blame as well. That is how one person's blame act becomes a culture. The study also cites that people with a high sense of self-worth tend to blame less and own more of their mistakes and actions.

But no matter what the excuse is, the result is the same: lack of ownership of your own story and the inability to author it. Life starts when we stop blaming others for our life.

Some of you will argue that some of the blame is justified and insist you have been wronged by others and that those people should be held accountable for their actions. You might be right. But in the big picture, your pursuit of blaming others (i.e., holding them accountable) prevents you from owning the part you can to transform it into a chapter you author.

Blaming and trying to hold people accountable is granting them power over your life story. It is a power they don't deserve.

In a previous chapter, we discussed COVID-19 and its effect on our lives. It is arguably the biggest helplessness-driving event most of us have experienced as individuals and as a collective world in our lifetime. Yet, we discussed how to own what we did and transform it into a chapter we are proud to add to our life story.

So even if you are eager to hold other people or circumstances accountable for your situation, ask yourself: at what price? What is the price you pay in giving up control of your life and the ability to move on with acceptance, understanding, and insight? In the grand scheme of things, move on and focus on your ownership and lessons. Let go of the blame. Those you are trying to hold accountable may never assume the responsibility you want to transfer to them, and you will lose valuable time you can use to develop your authored life story.

Focus on the power you have within the situation and own it. This is your version of the chapter you're authoring, and it should be developed around you and not others. It is time to change the arrow from pointing toward others to yourself. You are the owner of your life and the only author here.

But let me be clear: Anytime our story revolves around blaming others, we are not the authors of our story. We are not the heroes, but rather mere victims. We cannot author a story in which we are not the owners of our lives.

*Who should you stop blaming for authoring your story?*

## CHAPTER 23

# Reawaken the Inner Child

"Can you help me write the eulogy for my father?"

It was a strange request. I had never received one like it in my life. It was especially strange because it was from an old colleague we'll call Paul.

I liked Paul, but I do not do well with death. At that time, I had attended eight funerals in two years for close friends and family members. The notion of the end of life was heavily burdening me. I had also never written or given a eulogy before, and here was a request to write one for someone I had never met.

"The way you tell stories is amazing," Paul pressed. "And I want my eulogy for my father to sound like your stories."

What could I do?

I relented a bit, saying I couldn't write it, but I would be willing to review it and make some suggestions if he wanted to draft something. It felt like the right balance between authenticity (his story with his father) and some of the skills he asked me to activate for him.

I did give him a little advice before he got started: "Do not burden your audience with past stories that will only make them feel sadder and more helpless. Instead, highlight a characteristic of your father that was unique to him, something of his spirit you want to live on through the actions of people."

In short, I was asking Paul: What was your father's super-power? Why do we need more of it in the world?

"While most funerals leave you depressed and helpless," I said, "make this one a celebration of the impressive life he lived, with a beacon of hope for the future."

Paul sent me his proposed text and in it he identified his father's superpower as "reckless encouragement." Paul's father had the special skill of seeing beauty despite difficulty and encouraged people not to give up on their dreams and plans. He himself was able to do so even in the most desperate of situations, hence the recklessness. He was a God-fearing person who drew strength from the belief that God was on his side, even if he did not understand God's actions. This belief infused in him an inspiring strength of optimism that he shared with others.

I provided Paul with some suggestions to tweak and strengthen the message, to ensure the audience would be inspired rather than depressed. But then I realized something: a eulogy is a form of authoring one's life story. As I had listened to eulogies in the previous two years, I was thinking that they can be the best remedy for people who feel depressed, worthless, helpless. Hearing how much people loved and appreciated them might help someone find renewed strength to go through life's difficulties. It's a story of a life worth living, yet a eulogy is a story told too late.

In the story of Paul's father's reckless encouragement, I found something deeper. It connected me to the child within every one of us, the child born naïve and curious who sets off to discover the world. That child learns to dream and has been told that they can do anything they put their mind to. They draw pictures at four years old and demand that they be displayed proudly on the home's refrigerator. The child is full of hopes and aspirations. They can do anything. They are invincible, until they are not.

To become the dreamer instead of the firefighter, you need to reawaken your inner child. You were a dreamer when you were a child, and that still exists in all of us—but it's losing its voice. It's time to give the voice back.

## Listening to the Voice of Dreaming

When we were children, our parents provided us with reckless encouragement. They told us to pursue our dreams. But we didn't always.

The process of failures, mistakes, and denials slowly but constantly chipped away at our confidence and shrank our world of dreams to actions we knew we could do. We left behind new challenges, unknowns, and possibilities that could enrich and enliven our life story for the safety of the known. We stopped authoring new chapters and instead relived the greatest hits.

Life hits us with a harsh reality of "you don't belong here" rejections. But "mistakes" and "failures" are merely experiences not authored. They are still raw, with a potential negative impact on our life and future because we have not taken time to process and go through understanding, acceptance, and learning. When we do so, we free those experiences from their arresting negative impact and transform them into guiding posts.

The little dreaming child still lives in every one of us. Every so often, we hear her voice. That voice shrank in comparison with the size of our body and the magnitude of our life's challenges. We keep this small, naïve, pure voice inside. But we do not let it speak much. This voice is the voice of hope, despite disappointments. It is the voice of the possible in a field of impossibilities. It is the sole voice confronting a choir of "you can't."

What we want to do with this voice is our choice. That child is us in its purest form. Do we want to silence it or amplify it? Do we want to let it guide us, or do we want to become victims of circumstances?

The authoring process allows us to take external experiences and incorporate them into who we are uniquely, so the child can understand and relate, and we can keep dreaming.

If others around us, including Paul's father (may he rest in peace), are not around to give us reckless encouragement, we should do that for ourselves. We all deserve it. Dedicate the time to transform victimhood experiences into insightful guiding posts for the future journey. We will keep the child's voice strong (and dreaming) in our lives to author our life story.

*What failure of yours can use*
*some reckless encouragement?*

---

## CHAPTER 24

# Sharing the Imperfect Story

I was at the top of the Dubai Frame, a 150-meter structure designed to allow tourists to enjoy the view of Dubai. The view from the top was impressive, and the sun was setting. I noticed them coming out of the elevator: two teenage girls and their mother approaching the window and enjoying the view. As millions of tourists do everywhere, the charade started. One of the young girls assumed the perfect picture position with a thousand-watt smile. Her sister began to take pictures. A minute later she stopped, grabbed the phone from her sister, her smile disappearing as she checked the pictures on the smartphone. Unhappy with the results, she handed the phone back to her sister and again assumed the position. She later changed positions with her sister, who did the same as she had. As they left, I noticed something interesting: They never took a picture with their mother.

Remember the days when travel was a family experience we created together? Well, posed shots and "doing it for the 'gram" are not about family and togetherness. This is about living through the eyes of others, being validated and reassured by distributing fake images of perfection for the world to admire.

As I watched the girls smiling, it was clear to me that the expression on their face was merely a stretching of facial muscles and not a feeling deep in their hearts. Their faces and hearts were completely disconnected. Their life story at that moment was neither personal nor intimate. It was suspended, subject to the judgments of strangers and friends who would view their posted images and decide for themselves if this life story was interesting, exciting, and worth living. Like millions of others do, they outsourced their emotions to strangers and friends.

This is not living life. It is modeling life to some external standard. The absence of the mother from the picture taking was not a small mistake—it was symbolic. The mother would have ruined the image of youth and happiness they were trying to project. They may love their mother, but she didn't belong in the perfect image they attempted to convey to the world.

## The Danger of Living Picture-Perfect Moments

Addiction to social networks creates a false sense that we are documenting our authentic life and sharing it with others. But it's far from the truth. We share pictures of perfect slivers of life on Instagram, not real life. We do not express our full emotions but focus on crafting a false image of fun and excitement in a few seconds. It seems as if we are in a constant, never-ending, always evolving competition to live perfect lives. The world is not our oyster; it is our ultimate judgment.

By centering our lives around those fake-perfect moments, we downgrade the rest of our lives. We downplay the importance of the full spectrum of our events and emotions and let those linger unsolved and misunderstood. We divide our lives into moments we deem okay to post about on social networks (which reign supreme in our life priorities) and then the uninteresting moments (most of our life and the real part of it). The other moments become a burden in the journey of collecting likes on social networks. There could not be a bigger distortion of life by ignoring large swaths of it and subjecting the few remaining moments to the judgment of others.

Collecting pictures of yourself in fun and exciting situations, real or fake, is not authoring your life. It is exposing those events and your life to shallow, quick clicks. Here are the reasons why this is dangerous:

- The images you post are reflecting something other than what you might really feel at the moment (i.e., forced smiles).

- The images do not allow for depth and introspection.

- Living with those "always happy" images does not allow room to experience and express failures and pain.

- We end up ignoring most of our life.

- No lessons are developed from the experiences you have.

- The experiences are not becoming building blocks or milestones in a future journey.

- They are highly dependent on others' opinions, and there-fore do not reflect your true needs.

- They are not connected to the bigger story of your life.

- They do not express the true you.

Instead, moments you deem worthy are merely placed in your digital album. All you have is an image that doesn't even tell the real story, that is often forced and not truly linked to your emotions, character, and personality.

Even worse, you are not even sure if this moment is good or bad. You are merely serving your image for others to judge through their "likes," waiting for the verdict on whether your life is worth living or not.

When Facebook announced that they would allow users to erase posts, it was hugely welcomed. Now, you can erase a chapter of your life if people don't like it. You can keep the life story perfect, without the blemish of strangers' negative reactions.

Nothing can be more false than living life under the constant scrutiny of strangers, letting them determine what chapters of your life matter. It is the opposite of authoring your life story. It is the outsourcing of your life story to others. "What would my followers say?" becomes the center of your existence as you constantly feed them with more "perfect" images of your life.

## Sharing the Story and Development Process

I am spending time on this issue because it is so critical to dis-tinguish the fake from the real-life story authoring required.

Sharing your life story with others is empowering—if done right. It is a great way to create context, share life lessons, and stay connected to family, friends, and society. But what you should be sharing is far from the "perfect smile" Instagram images. The images I'm talking about are ones where the smile is real, and the mother is included.

We live our lives alone and in the context of others. Often, our own emotions about a certain experience are a result of someone else saying something. It can be an argument with a loved one or a discussion at work. Other people are often actors in our life story. Exploring their side of the story can add depth and understanding to your own chapter's development. It is likely that you have perceived their role and reaction differently than what they truly meant. It doesn't invalidate your chapters, but it does add more dimension, and hopefully, understanding and insights. Getting other people's perspective on the events can be extremely useful, providing additional color and clarity as to what happened and how they saw your role in it.

Authoring your life should not be a personal "My Diary" exercise. Those are often subjective and focus on extreme emotions. Because they are isolated, these sessions fail to allow you to develop life lessons and instead focus on discussing scars from disappointments. Engaging others on the other side opens the opportunity to fully develop understanding of the chapter and create a fuller picture of what happened (and the meaning of your experience).

Sharing lessons with others is another way of exposing your life story to others. As you reach new wisdom and insights, this becomes especially rewarding. Friends and family may benefit from knowing you have experienced a similar situation. I call it "reality check reassurance." Sometimes the mere fact that I am not alone, and others have had similar fears or doubts, can be very empowering. It can help me move to action and away from being paralyzed by fear. In other cases, your life lessons can stir others toward making better, more educated decisions. Nothing can be more powerful than using your life lessons to help others. Share them instead of a fake smile.

*Who would you share your life story with?*

*What would they learn from your life story?*

## CHAPTER 25

# Your Story's Center of Gravity

When I feel stuck and helpless, I reach out to a friend who I know is not doing well and send them an encouraging message. It can be a friend I haven't spoken to for a while or who is going through a transition or difficult chapter in his journey. It is a practice I started when I realized that even in my worst moments, there is something I can give to others. Giving makes me feel great. It makes me feel full and not empty, and the feeling of helplessness is less painful.

For it is in giving that we receive.

—Saint Francis of Assisi

The sole meaning of life is to serve humanity.

—Leo Tolstoy

Giving back is as good for you as it is for those you are
helping, because giving gives you purpose. When you have
a purpose-driven life, you are a happier person.

—Goldie Hawn[1]

Research throughout the years has established the premise
that helping others is a source of personal happiness. A study
published in *The Journal of Positive Psychology* titled "Happiness
Comes from Trying to Make Others Feel Good, Rather Than
Oneself" attempts to answer why.[2] Conducting five different
studies, the researchers concluded that trying to make others
happy resulted in greater happiness to the giver as opposed to
other ways to make oneself happy. Their fifth study tested this
idea by having subjects feed other people's parking meters without engaging the people. The results demonstrated that even
without interacting with the people they helped, the subjects'
sense of well-being was heightened. According to the study's
findings, people's happiness is often tied to creating connections
with others. By helping others, we develop links to other people
and enrich our social lives—and, therefore, our happiness.

But is helping others merely a means to an end? If the answer
is yes, I doubt it will develop long-term, authentic happiness. It
would be more like a cynical attempt to develop connections for
selfish reasons, which defeats the whole purpose. The way helping others is marketed by speakers and writers everywhere as a
quick fix will lead to fast disappointment if the intent doesn't
have deeper roots.

In the Jewish tradition, there is a strong emphasis on *tzedakah*, most commonly translated as "charity." The root of the word *tze-dakah* is *tzedek*, which means "justice." In Judaism, charity is not just a matter of good hearts helping others. It goes deeper, representing a form of mutual responsibility to each other and the community. While charity is often perceived as voluntary, charity based on the principle of *tzedakah* is mandatory. It reminds every person that the center of the universe is not themselves but the community, with a commitment and responsibility to others.

When I discovered this rule, I found it surprising that even poor people were required to give *tzedakah*. Considering that the amount a poor person can give is so small that it will hardly make a difference, why require them to give? The answer is quite simple: they are giving to belong to the communal responsibility. They give partly in order to center their life's gravity on others. By doing so, this grants them the possibility of happiness and purpose.

The impact of giving on the giver was explored in a fascinating article in *Harvard Medicine* magazine titled "What We Get When We Give." The authors cite multitudes of research indicating the power of giving on people's happiness and life expectancy.[3]

This profound idea is that the act of giving serves both the recipient and the giver within a communal belonging, and responsibility transforms the giver into a receiver as well. Life's purpose is not defined by how much money you have, but rather by what you do with it and who you care for. In that regard, the richest and poorest people are equal when they give *tzedakah*. They both gain a center of gravity from seeing and caring for the other, and by demonstrating a communal responsibility.

## Discovering a Center of Gravity

What is your center of gravity? Do you exist to stratify yourself or to make an impact on others? Are you seeking purpose and happiness by delighting yourself or by developing others? Do you help others merely to serve your needs for satisfaction, making yourself the center of gravity? Or is the center of gravity others, with you there to help them? If it's the latter, then you may draw a more authentic and lasting sense of satisfaction.

Now that you have authored several chapters of your life story, you can start detecting a theme. Review those chapters and ask yourself:

- What were the main lessons you learned about yourself from those chapters?

- What insights did you discover about your superpower?

- What was the role of others in your story? Were they major or supporting actors?

- In the chapters where you drew the most satisfaction and happiness, what was your role versus the role of others?

- In the chapters where you experienced the most sadness and unhappiness, what was your role versus the roles of others?

- What was your approach to those other people? Were you trying to get things out of them or give them something?

As your story develops, it is an opportunity to start identifying the patterns and understanding your center of gravity. Is your story a lonely one or one of social connections? In social connections, are you the recipient or the provider?

There's nothing wrong with being the recipient. We all have things we need from others and can learn in the process. But over time, we want to start shifting the balance and evolve to be providers and not just takers. It may take some time to discover what we can give back. But remember, for a lonely person, a simple smile or message at the right time can go a long way to provide them with hope. We all have something to give, even in our worst moments.

Authoring your life story does not have to focus on the "your" as a selfish dependent and taker self. It can easily focus on the "story," the one you create for yourself through interactions and engagement with others. It can be a story of providing and creating an impact, making others the center of gravity as they benefit from your commitment and willingness to help.

The act of the author is first and foremost sincere. It's authentic. It does not seek quick fixes or cynical giving for quick gratification. The goal is outlining a road map to recognizing the beauty in our lives, and constantly making the map more powerful and purposeful. The best stories of life are the ones that place the impact we make on others as the center of gravity, and us as committed providers to a greater good.

*Who is placed at the center of your story's gravity?*

## CHAPTER 26

# Lead with Your Personal Story

We were backstage at one of the largest hotel ballrooms in Las Vegas, getting ready to go on stage. It was the annual conference for a global company. We were all set to go with makeup, connected microphones, and presentations ready. After hours of rehearsals, it was showtime.

The CEO turned to me and said, "You need to teach me how to speak on stage. You always get it right and the audience loves you." (Not sure I agree, but that is beside the point.)

I replied, "I can teach you right now."

"Really?" he asked. "How?"

"When did you first fall in love with this company's product?" I asked. "Why are you so proud to work here? Start your presentation not with slides and numbers. Shut down the PowerPoint and start by looking at your audience and telling them your story. Your personal story, not your corporate story. Tell them the answer to both questions."

"Why would they care?"

"Just trust me."

He was puzzled. But he did trust me.

During his story, you could hear a pin drop. He received a standing ovation at the end, for the first time in his life.

People lead people. PowerPoints do not. Your personal story is your most powerful tool to lead people.

What is leadership? We all know by now it is not to command and control. It is not a top-down approach to getting things done. Ultimately, leadership is raising people to their highest level of performance. It is providing them with the confidence, tools, and support to deliver at the highest standards, to innovate, create, deliver, and exceed objectives.

Before you establish a purpose, document the vision, mission, and values; or establish measurable objectives—you must start by connecting with people. That connection is your personal story.

## The Story That Leads People

By authoring your story, you create a more ready-to-share version of your experience, a version that is well understood, fully accepted, and already has lessons determined. Your story is no longer a sob story in search of pity and tears. It is a story of resilience and courage, with insights and lessons that others can relate to and learn from.

This is the power of authoring in the context of leadership. It does not matter if you are a CEO with formal power or a team member with informal power trying to get your team to make a certain decision. Your personal story will enable you to connect with people and sway them in your direction.

When sharing your story, it does not mean you need to strip it down to the most embarrassing version. You need to share a story that will be authentically human and uniquely you, but also effective. It should not burden people with your pain but lift them to your gain. A well-authored story is distilled down to its inspiration with less desperation.

Leadership is about making choices. We demonstrate who we are and what we stand for not by what we write, but rather by the decisions we make. Asking other people to take certain actions is asking them to make choices and actively stand for something. That is where your authored story comes into play. People follow people. More accurately, people follow people's actions. There is no better way to demonstrate your intentions and vision than by demonstrating the choices you made in the past (as you ask others to make a choice). It establishes you as a true leader of action, not just words.

Sharing your personal story is not a method of touchy-feely engagement. It is a demonstration that you do what you ask others to do. More importantly, it shows that you understand the difficulties and pain that those choices may require. Our authored story is the ultimate role modeling.

## How Should a Leader Share Their Story?

Like other forms of storytelling, your story needs to connect to the audience emotionally and not just rationally. It cannot be a dry description of a problem and solution. Take the time to really tell it to your people. Consider this checklist of personal stories that, when shared at the right time with the right message, can create an authentic leadership narrative that will make your team want to follow you:

- A threat or difficulty you faced

- The choices you were considering during the threat or difficulty

- The fears you were experiencing during the consideration

- The other voices you heard during deliberation

- The power you didn't have and the sense of helplessness you experienced

- The courage you mustered to make a decision and/or take action

- The risk you took to make the decision

- The ultimate outcome following your taking action

- The lessons you learned

- What you would recommend to someone in a similar situation

Remember, this needs to be both an effective and emotionally connecting story. It is not an exercise in vulnerability for the sake of it. You can drop unnecessary details, but make sure to share the ones that can make the story more alive (such as place, time, names of people, your role, and other relatable details). For example, if this was about your first job out of college and you made that choice despite all the challenges, some of the junior members of your team may find this helpful. They may recognize that they have permission to lead right now and not in a decade. This leadership may inspire people to rise to a level of performance they never knew they had.

## Stories and the Power to Rise

As you share your story and see the impact it makes on people, you will recognize how powerful your authoring has become. The story will serve as a center of gravity, in which others are the impacted individuals of your experience. This amplifies the power of your story and your purpose.

There is nothing more gratifying than to help people reach new heights. We all read about coaches who lead failing teams to championships and wins that they never dreamed of accomplishing. Your story is a superpower to do just this with the people around you. Share it with family members, direct reports, friends, and colleagues. Just beware of coming across as bragging and arrogant. When shared authentically, the impact of your story will transform your personal pain into many people's gains.

*What story conveys your*
*personal leadership skills best?*

## CHAPTER 27

# Authoring Your
# Work Story with Purpose

I t started as a trickle in April 2021 and ended up as a massive movement by August. At that point, over forty million Americans had resigned from their jobs, without having necessarily lined up the next one. "The Great Resignation" was arguably one of the largest self-initiated movements of employees against employers in the last century.

But this wasn't the end. It was followed by additional waves of employee-initiated actions, including "quiet quitting" (the art of phasing out work until you work as little as possible), "acting your wage" (the art of refusing to work after five o'clock or to take on additional tasks), and "application rage" (the art of immediately applying for another job when your boss upsets you). These four major movements in the span of less than four years sent a message to the world of work and employment.[1]

In short, the old contract between employees and employers where employees were supposed to shut up and do their work in exchange for a financial package that would pay their bills and for some of their leisure activities—it was broken. Employees rebelled in droves and exclaimed, "Not anymore."

In a post–COVID-19 world, we are all rethinking our priorities and what we would be willing to sacrifice for. We're examining our relationships. Society-wide isolation allowed for a period of reflection, and employer–employee relationships were reflected on and seen anew. It used to be that people joined companies but left bosses. Disagreement, lack of growth opportunities, and lack of chemistry were the number one drive for people switching jobs. This is no longer the case. Humans are now looking for purpose, not only in their personal lives but in their nine-to-five.[2] If their workplace did not live by their values, they quit or went into autopilot to do the minimum.

## From the Wall to the Soul

Every company spends time and effort developing their mission, vision, values, and purpose. The problem is that most believe it's sufficient to place those on the wall and move on.

I recall once spending time with a company where their mission was to make it simple for their customers to do business with them. Signs stating that goal were posted all over the offices. But their actual performance was anything but. It turned out, they found that making it difficult for customers to work with them was more profitable. Yes. Believe it or not, they made money from customers' misery.

What employees are demanding is a simple reality check. Move the purpose and values from the wall to the soul. Move the values from a forgotten PowerPoint presentation to the actual way you make decisions and create tradeoffs. Employees are simply calling BS on this charade. They want an authentic commitment to purpose that is translated into day-to-day decisions, behaviors, and performance. In the absence of those, they feel a clash between their personal values and those of the organization and refuse to accept living this way. The old employee–employer contract places financial compensation as the primary vehicle of the relationship. Today, employees are willing to trade that financial compensation for purpose fulfillment. (Money is still important but no longer the absolute.)

We all work. It's a big part of our life, so we need to incorporate it and not separate it. It's not about work-life balance—it's all life. We need to incorporate our job as part of our story, not just think of it as a way to pay the bills.

## Rethinking Purpose at Work

If you have been to a museum, you know that there are different types of visitors.

- **Type 1 Visitors: "Passive"**—the visitors who show up to buy tickets, walk around quietly, and hope to be entertained by the exhibit. They are passive, occasionally take pictures, and move rather quickly from one painting to the other.

- **Type 2 Visitors: "Interested"**—the visitors who rent the audio guide and stop to listen to the story behind each painting.

- **Type 3 Visitors: "Dialogue"**—the groups. They show up with a guide who not only explains the narrative but is open to questions and conducts a dialogue that includes the group members' reflections and feelings.

- **Type 4 Visitors: "Invested"**—they come prepared. These visitors have researched the exhibit, and they know what they are looking for. Sometimes they may stay and draw one of the images or participate in a special workshop. They take professional pictures, and they are excited.

These types, which I recently observed during visits to several museums in Paris such as the Centre Pompidou, Musée d'Orsay, and the Musée des Impressionnismes Giverny (the home of Claude Monet), are an illustration of how we connect ideas and values. Passive visitors approach the museum with an attitude of "Entertain me. Show me the money." They have little invested and hardly engage, yet they expect magic to happen to them. Invested guests, on the other hand, understand that nothing will happen unless they act. There is no experience unless you are invested and engaged. They make the experience interesting. Their attitude is "It is on me."

I would like to propose that the same is true with values and purpose in the workplace. Except for organizations that are deliberately hurting customers (which I believe the vast majority are not), most organizations attempt to conduct business in a way that creates value for their customers and brings their purpose to life. But there is no way to bring purpose in a vague, centralized way from the top down. The purpose comes to life from people's decisions and actions. Every employee's decision matters. Every customer interaction matters. The sum total of employees' choices creates the organization's story (and ultimately, success).

The expectation of "make the purpose work for me or I leave" is the passive visitor's attitude and will not work. If you approach purpose at the workplace as something that will happen to you, but not with you and by you, you are likely to be disappointed fast. (The same is true for life as well.) According to studies, as many as 80 percent of those who quit their job during the Great Resignation regretted their decision.[3] It didn't live up to their expectations. One of the reasons, among others, was that they treated purpose as a passive exercise that needs to be done for them.

You want to live a purposeful life in the workplace? Make it happen. Participate. Get invested.

You might be thinking, "But I am not the CEO." Think again. For every action you make, there is a customer on the other side. A customer who has dreams, hopes, fears, and aspirations. A customer who will live with the consequences of your work. For that customer, YOU are the CEO.

You must now decide to deliver an exceptional, infused-with-purpose performance or just deliver the basics. Your choice is between delivering an awesome product or a mediocre one. Living with purpose in the workplace is not waiting for the annual volunteering day arranged by the head of ESG or human resources. Living with purpose is weaving it into everything you do. It is choosing to act as an invested visitor and not a passive one. Choose to be an impact creator, not just a process follower.

Purpose in the workplace will happen when thousands of employees make millions of purposeful decisions that will be infused with values and passion. This is how purpose moves from the wall to the soul. The CEO can't be there for every decision you make. She can have a vision and a path, but the rest is on you.

The personal purpose and corporate purpose may seem in conflict to you. But I would like you to reflect: What have you done to bring the purpose to life? What power do you have to make purpose a reality in your scope of work? If you start, it will be contagious, and others will follow.

In short, if you want purpose in the workplace, make it happen. Look at the eyes of your customers (physically or metaphorically) and start realizing how much power you have to make their lives better, more exciting, or less painful.

*What are you doing to activate your purpose?*

CHAPTER 28

# Stories Create
# Exceptional Performance

Arguably one of the most powerful examples of a performance-defining event for a company was done by a chain-smoking, alcohol-drinking CEO. His actions shaped performance for years at his company, and his employees loved it. In fact, he decorated the company's locations with pictures from the event to remind them all about the story and its message to every employee.

This is the story of "Malice in Dallas," and in typical corporate world style, it started with a legal dispute that led to a lawsuit.

It all started when Stevens Aviation sued Southwest Airlines for trademark infringement for using their slogan "Just Plane Smart." Herb Kelleher, the Southwest Airlines CEO and protagonist of this story, was a lawyer by training and responded to the lawsuit in an unusual way. He invited the Stevens Aviation

CEO to an arm-wrestling contest. Kelleher did not know that Stevens Aviation's CEO Kurt Herwald was a bodybuilder. Herwald did not fully appreciate Kelleher's leadership style. Both sides accepted.

Kelleher booked the Dallas Sportatorium, a major stadium, and invited employees and press to the event. He jokingly "trained" for the event by smoking and lifting bottles of bourbon while watching Muhammad Ali's videos. In the spirit of pro wrestling, he showed up in full regalia and was welcomed by thousands of employees who cheered him on from their seats. To enhance the story, he competed while smoking a cigarette. He lost in two out of the three matches. But despite the loss, Stevens Aviation received so much free publicity from the event that they let it go, eventually settling with Southwest and allowing them to use the slogan.

Legal fights are long, expensive, and usually result in both sides feeling cheated. They never end well. For a company with a promise of great customer service, going forward with a lawsuit would have been the wrong move. Kelleher did something else to send a message to all his current employees and future employees as well: Southwest does it differently. They showed that they do not follow the beaten path. They sought quick and fun ways to resolve disputes, and to do things in a way that is easier, cheaper, and more fun for all involved.

Kelleher knew that the power of story is far greater than any corporate memo he could issue with the same message. This is why he kept pictures surrounding the story in every office. The story will live on and reinforce the company's values, a far greater building block in the corporate culture.

## The Power of Stories to Shape Reality

During a nationwide transformation project for a major car manufacturer, I gave each branch a quota of creating five shareable stories in sixty days. I wanted them to create the stories and then document them and share them with other branches, especially ones that embodied the company's commitment to customers. The stories had to be real and authentic, exceed expectations, and surprise the customers.

We collected over five thousand stories in less than a year. During the process of documentation, we videotaped many of the participants and shared them publicly with all the branches. By documenting the stories, we created an inspiration and a support mechanism that enabled employees to tell their stories. It inspired employees to think big but also provided a safety net that made them feel secure in daring to create future stories.

The CEO's response? "I didn't know they could perform at that level."

I was not surprised. Most employees want to do an amazing job and be proud of their work. But a company culture with a lack of inspiring stories usually has employees stick to formulated manuals that require them to perform to strict guidelines. The overall performance becomes blandly consistent, boring, and undifferentiated for customers. Only with inspiration, permission, and encouragement will employees bring their personal touch and creativity to wow customers.

Stories are a source of inspiration and living proof that the company lives up to the values, purpose, and mission that it took upon itself. As we discussed in the previous chapter, purpose is not what is on the wall. It is what is in the soul. The soul of the organization is their decisions, behavior, and actions. By creating inspiring stories, we give permission to perform exceptionally.

As a leader, your role is to remove obstacles and help your team members rise to higher levels of performance. Sometimes that obstacle is not physical, but mental—employees do not believe they have permission to perform at those standards. Create stories that will inspire them to do so.

Herb Kelleher knew that he could not be in every customer interaction or guide employees to the best resolution to a dispute. But his stories can be there, whispering how to do things the Southwest way.

## Stories at the Moment of Truth

It was the ultimate freak accident in consulting. One of our consultants conducted a focus group at a branch of a Fortune 500 services company. The employees participated to gather insight and assist the branch in improving its performance. But one of the participants, against the original agreement, decided to talk about another participant who spoke badly about the branch manager. Fuming, the branch manager fired the employee who spoke badly about him on the spot and held my consultant accountable for a "coup" in his branch. He also threatened to escalate the situation to the company's CEO and demand that we be fired.

It was a moment of truth. We did not have much time to plan a story. The episode was evolving in front of our faces.

One of my colleagues (who was a veteran of one of the big four consulting firms) suggested we go the route of his previous employer. He suggested we fire the consultant and blame her for not following the rules, to isolate the situation and distance ourselves from it. I called the consultant to debrief. She actually had followed the rules, and not only that, the insights she had gathered about the branch manager were real. It was simply that the branch manager felt threatened by what was discovered and lashed out, a typical situation in our line of work. I decided we would stick by this consultant, as she had done nothing wrong, and try to fix things with our client. It would be no small feat, but I was determined to stick by our value: "Always do the human thing first."

I personally reached out to the branch manager and had a heart-to-heart discussion with him. I was respectful of the manager's experience and expertise, but firm about the call for action I requested. The fired employee was rehired, and the project was brought back on track.

That consultant shared that story with others in the organization, and it became a legend. She was sure we would fire her and distance ourselves. It would have been the easy way out. But instead, we stuck by her. It inspired many of our consultants for years to come. Our people know that we have their backs when they work on difficult transformation projects. We will not side with clients, especially if the clients are wrong. I still remember that moment and the decision we had to make. I was afraid that I would lose the project. I was not sure what would be the ultimate outcome. But the decision to stick with our consultant was in line with our company's values, and everyone thereafter knew that this value was real. It became part of our storybook, and a guide for everyone else to follow.

Organizations are not a pile of manuals and legal warnings. They are a set of stories and chapters written every day. Author them, document them, and share them to create the culture and behavior you want. Culture is what happens when the leader leaves the room. The stories they share are the true story of your company, much more powerful than sweeping statements. They are also the true predictors of future behavior of your employees, while manuals and procedures are escape routes for employees not to deliver their best. Stories are the inspirational accelerators to help your employees reach an exceptional level of performance.

*Which story from your company provides*
*permission to perform exceptionally?*

## CHAPTER 29

# The Stories of Relationships

R elationships are stories in progress. Our spectrum of relationships is diverse. Some of those relationships are chosen by us, and others are forced upon us. We do not choose our parents or our children, but we do choose our friends, our lovers, and eventually our spouses, and those relationships are more under our control (until they are not).

Relationships are always full of drama, as two authors of separate stories try to connect and craft a mutual chapter that fits into both of their life stories. If there was ever a definition of too many cooks in the kitchen, this is it. Not only is there more than one cook laboring in the kitchen, trying to control things and taking up space, but they often use different recipes (or at least different versions of recipes) to try to create togetherness and mutual happiness.

I do not know too many books written by two or more authors. It does happen sometimes when a ghostwriter is helping a primary author bring his or her thoughts to life. Sometimes two researchers publish a study they labored on together. But by and large, a book with more than one author is an anomaly. Books are most often written by one author who conceives a vision, translates it into words and narrative, and publishes it.

This is not how relationship stories are written.

It is difficult to write your life story and find understanding, acceptance, and lessons for events you encounter alone. The challenge is magnified significantly when you author relationship stories. You may already see how it's hard to find that understanding and common ground with forced relationships, such as between parents and children. Here is why:

- Each author brings a unique vantage point to the story.

- Each author brings a unique purpose to the story.

- Each author's previous story includes chapters not always known (or understood) by the other author.

- Each author will experience the relationships differently from an emotional standpoint.

- Each author may bring different expectations to the relationship.

- Each author brings different approaches and tools to solve problems.

- Each author defines happiness differently.

- Each author's tolerance to challenges will be different.

- Each author will reflect differently on joint events.

- Each author will draw different lessons from the joint events.

In short, different perspectives and expectations are trying to join forces and create beauty together. It is tough. But it can be beautiful if done with a shared commitment in mind.

## It's about Raising, Not Erasing

One of the biggest risks in relationship stories is that one person will erase their authentic self to please the other. It happens at an early age, when children entertain their parents' wishes and try to please them. But erasing oneself can only end in resentment. In relationships between lovers, we commonly hear about one person erasing their true self to be the person their lover wants. We discussed the pleasing phenomena in previous chapters and mentioned its damaging effects. In a long-term relationship, the damage may go beyond one event and into a complete diversion from one's own self and story. We start to craft an inauthentic story of a version we think others want us to be.

Needless to say (and research backs this up), pleasing others at the expense of oneself is a destructive behavior.[1] From an authoring standpoint, it may produce cautionary tales but not real chapters that belong in your life story (unless of course you want it to be the cautionary tale that taught you not to do that).

Relationships are not about erasing; they are about raising. Togetherness should produce a *better person* individually, not a *different* one.

In my discussions with leaders, I define the role of the leader as someone who helps people rise to the better version of themselves (often to a version that person didn't know existed). A great leader creates an environment that supports employees fostering the daring to dream, courage to try, resilience to fail, and commitment to continue pursuing the goal. This kind of relationship respects the self but firmly challenges it to grow and develop. This is true for every relationship.

What can change are the versions of you that you bring to people. Every relationship is a chemical reaction between you and the other person. In my relationships, I have friends who always bring out cynical voices in me and so that is the version of me that is unveiled during meetings and discussions with them. With other friends, the chemical reaction creates an optimistic person spreading words of hope. I am the same person, but different interactions create different versions of me that respond to the other person's authentic self. Have you ever noticed that about yourself? Have you recognized how some people bring out the best in you, while others leave you feeling deflated and uninspired? We all have those relationships. Why? Because they are not authored relationships.

That is why authoring in relationships is so critical. It determines which chapter you write in the future, through the experience of choosing to sustain and grow relationships and abandoning those that develop a version of you that you wish to minimize.

Even in forced relationships such as parents, children, or family members, the authoring process enables you to discover what version of yourself each relationship creates. You can then develop strategies to better those relationships or minimize their negative influence on you. When authoring relationship stories, consider the following questions:

The Stories of Relationships  |  223

- Is this a relationship you chose or were forced into?

- What do conversations with this person look like?

- How do you feel when interacting with that person?

- What version of you does the interaction with that person create?

- How do you feel about this person?

- In what way, if any, does the relationship allow you to grow and develop?

- How do you feel after interacting with the person?

- Do you find yourself being more yourself or morphing into an unauthentic version of you?

- Are you in the relationship because you must be, or because you want to be?

- Do you try hard to please and obtain validation from the other person?

- Do you find yourself craving more or less time with that person?

- Why are you in a relationship with the person?

These questions should help guide you to understand what version of yourself a certain relationship creates, and how to assess staying in the relationship via the version of you it creates. If you are your authentic self while also growing and developing and you crave more time with that person, that relationship sounds like a wonderful chapter that ought to be part of your life story. If it is not, then time to reassess.

Relationships are a story in progress. Another author is involved, who will craft their version of joint events. That chapter will be different from yours. But the story ought to be both authentically yours and lead you to a better version of yourself as a result of the relationship. The chapter that tells the relationship's story should tell a story of a better person as a result, rather than that of a person that would have pursued his or her goals alone. Those are the best chapters, where another person is your biggest cheerleader and personal trainer leading you to new triumphs.

*What version of you does one*
*of your relationships create?*

CHAPTER 30

# Your Story—Growing Old or Growing Young?

Benjamin Franklin invented the bifocal lens at the age of seventy-eight. Frank Lloyd Wright designed the Guggenheim Museum at the age of ninety-two. Claude Monet painted his famous water lilies in his mid-eighties. These are just a few examples of innovations and creativity that burst forth in people's later years.

Why did they wait so long to make their breakthroughs? How come those creations didn't happen earlier?

In his book *Old Masters and Young Geniuses*, David Galenson describes two types of innovators: conceptual and experimental.[1] Conceptual innovators, such as Mozart, tend to do their best work in their early years. Experimental innovators, on the other hand, do their best work in their later years. They grow by trial and error and produce better, more distilled ideas after a journey of failures and mistakes.

As we develop our story in a deliberate fashion, the question is: where will it lead us? Will the lessons learned produce experimental innovations? Or do we grow old and live off our early years' innovations and successes?

The answer to this question, I would argue, is a matter of choice. As we advance our life story and accumulate experience, insights, and lessons, the question becomes: to what end? What is our purpose for this deliberate story development? Authoring our life story is ultimately a choice to convert our life experiences into resilience and strength that will elevate our next chapters to an impactful performance we will be proud of. It is a choice to live a more meaningful life.

## Different Approaches to Growth through Stories

As we examine the best way to utilize our stories, there are several paths you can take to apply them. There are four primary characters of story applications:

1. Perspective providers

2. Generation connectors

3. Purpose seekers

4. Growing innovators

Perspective providers are people who choose to transform their story into a perspective to share with new employees, children, or grandchildren. They want to provide wisdom that makes life easier to live and perspective that will enable the next generation to live better. When a young child or employees confront a difficulty that seems unimaginable and unconquerable, perspective providers offer a story from the past that will have a similar threat or difficulty. They share how ultimately, with the perspective of time, a trial wasn't all bad. In some cases, it even resulted in a surprising outcome, or all worked out for the best.

For others, the role of the evolving story is to connect generations to an eternal purpose. The purpose can be a set of values, religion, or family continuity. Generation connectors will demonstrate how their life story strengthens the goal for the next generation. All suffering, difficulties, and pains will be considered worthy sacrifices for the purpose of connecting the generations. When a younger family member or professional approaches them with a challenge, the greater goal of connecting generations and leaving a legacy will be at the center of their story to illustrate the path forward for the future.

Purpose seekers use their story to infuse a sense of meaning into every event. They transform happenings into purposeful experiences by seeking to demonstrate that nothing is random, and everything has a meaning. When a young family member or a colleague shares a certain situation, they will identify a story from their repository in which the inciting event initially seems random. But at the end, the episode was full of meaning and created an impact. As such, they will advise the younger generation to seek purpose in everything they do.

Each of the storyteller characters ages, but each uses their story to grow old in their own way. They transform themselves over the years from doers to wise guides. At a certain point, their stories of creation stop and transform into stories of wisdom to be shared with younger people at the optimal time in their development. The stories stop growing and become part of a library.

I am pointing out this transformation without judgment. Younger generations lean on the wisdom of older generations to avoid mistakes, build on their past successes, and provide a sense of belonging, continuity, and purpose.

It is a choice to transform your story into one of these story-as-wisdom characters. It's a good choice, as long as you evolve away from the creator and into the role of a guide. This transition requires grace, full awareness, and acceptance.

The last character, the growing innovator, is radically different. While this person can share perspective, connection, or purpose with others, they are predominantly busy with continuing to create. Their story is not wisdom to be shared. It is refined knowledge used to create better. They do not stop the acts of innovation, creation, and growth. They use their story as a building block for a better knowledge base—a smarter one to improve innovations for the world. Franklin, Wright, and Monet made the choice to continue and create throughout their lives. They refused to settle on being wisdom storytellers and insisted on staying creator storytellers.

## How Will You Choose?

The choice between wisdom storyteller and creator storyteller is directly related to the way we process our stories. It also centers on the lessons we insist on drawing from them and how we file them in our minds. Consider the following questions as you reflect on the choice:

- When an event is turning into a life story, how actionable are your insights?

- Do those insights lead you to repeat the event later (but in a better way) or to let it go?

- When you review your life story lessons, do they lead to motivation toward more or less acceptance of success?

- Are your life story lessons easily transferable to others or uniquely yours?

- Are you crafting insights ready to share or to keep them personal?

As you review the insights and lessons you gather throughout writing your chapters, you will discover that they will naturally fall into one of two categories: driving lessons or closure lessons. Driving lessons are ones you can apply to do better next time around. Closure lessons close the chapter with you feeling satisfied and proud but not acting beyond that. Driving lessons are open chapters establishing the next chapter. Closure lessons are designed to reach satisfaction.

If you wish to make the choice to become a growing innovator, you need to seek different lessons from your life story. Focus on questions such as:

- What worked?

- What didn't work?

- Why didn't it work?

- Now that I know what I know, how would I do it differently and better?

- When would I try again?

If you want to create closure, those questions would be—

- How do I feel about it?

- What was the purpose of it?

- What impact did I create?

As your story grows in insight, it will evolve to serve a purpose. You will either become a wisdom storyteller or a growing innovator-style storyteller. Consider your choice carefully, then author your lessons accordingly.

*What lessons are you drawing from your life story?*
*What kind of storyteller does it make you?*

CHAPTER 31

# It's a Choice (Even if It Doesn't Feel That Way)

There is always a choice.
Holocaust survivor and famous founder of logo-therapy Viktor Frankl discusses a tough question at the end of his book *Man's Search for Meaning*: How can one trust humanity after the horrors created by humans during the Holocaust?[1]

His conclusion was quite simple. You can choose to have the oppressors depict humanity, or you can view the victims who marched to their death while saying their prayers to be the representatives of humanity. There is always a choice.

Authoring your life is a choice.

It does not mean that life will always go according to your plans.

It does not mean that you will be in full control during your life.

It does not mean that people will always be nice to you.

It does not mean that tragedies will not happen.

It does not mean that life is all rainbows and happiness.

It does not mean that your children will always agree with you.

It does not mean your spouse will always be happy.

It does not mean your boss will promote you.

It does not mean your colleagues will always appreciate your contributions.

It does not mean that everyone will like you.

It does not mean you will always be healthy.

It does not mean that all your wishes will come true.

It does not mean you will have all the money you wish for.

Yet, you do have a choice.

Not just the choice of how to react to what is happening to you.

It is the choice to author it and weave it into your life story.

There is a difference. Choosing your reaction is nice and often done reluctantly, as if to say, "I wish it hadn't happened. But now that it has, let me make the most of it." It is a reactive approach to try to make lemonade out of the lemon when deep down, you would have preferred a mango.

## Authoring Is Distinctly Proactive

Authoring is a proactive approach to turning life experiences into celebrated chapters and milestones. It is embracing our life events and infusing meaning into them. But beyond simply infusing purpose into the past, authoring is converting those experiences into future strength and resilience that prepares you to be triumphant in your next challenge. In authoring life, we are seeking to craft a deeper meaning out of life occurrences and transform our stories into layers of strength and learnings that enrich our lives. Authoring is seeking a higher purpose—your purpose.

Authoring a painful event is refusing to be a victim. It is a process of discovering the strengths and capabilities within you, to not only survive a painful event but thrive.

During COVID-19, I was approached by many clients asking how to navigate this phenomenon that had arrived at everyone's footsteps. We were all without any manual or historical lesson to leverage.

My first question was, "What are you trying to do, survive or thrive?"

Almost unanimously, people would ask, "What kind of thriving are you talking about? Aren't we all out here just trying to survive right now?"

The pandemic came without an expiration date, manual, relevant experience, government guidelines, or anything else for us to follow.

Those were the prevailing feelings . . . but they weren't exactly true. They didn't allow for past insights to guide our future. We thought we were stuck in an unwritten story chapter, devoid of context and tools to decipher its unknown nature and develop a path forward—but that's just the story we told ourselves. These feelings ignored our past experiences and life story chapters. The answers were actually in us the whole time.

My challenge for these clients was to thrive. If we're going to work hard, let's work hard toward thriving and not simply surviving. Everyone has a strategy until they get punched in the face. Well, my clients and their competitors were all punched in the face. The question was, who would get up better and create new opportunities?

With this mindset we reflected on how different companies experienced other global events such as 9/11 and the 2008 financial crisis. What did the company learn from those global events? How did your organization respond? What were the strengths that allowed you to evolve and survive?

What we were doing was simply authoring past chapters, to transform them from being a forgotten past into a current strength. Make no mistake, those reflections were not all easy or comfortable. They were painful, sometimes requiring a postmortem of mistakes and decisions that went awry. The process was one of understanding, acceptance, and learning that required emotional and intelligent maturity. But it was required to find guidance for the future. We found answers to questions such as:

- How do we make decisions in a crisis?

- What needs to be involved?

- How do we implement this during a crisis?

- What was effective and what was not?

- How do we engage employees into execution during a crisis?

- How do we communicate with all stakeholders during a crisis?

- What values will be evaluated during crisis times?

- What tools were most effective during a crisis?

- What should leadership's role be during a crisis?

These universal questions were answered very differently by different companies. Not all of them managed to change the same way. Their cultures dictated different responses, some more effective than others. The fact that we needed to author those chapters fifteen to twenty years after a major event happened was difficult because many of the people involved were no longer with the company. That is why authoring needs to be formally documented closer to when events take place, to make sure we capture all relevant information and lessons.

Eventually, in working with these clients, the process resulted in recognizing the contribution of life-changing events to the company's story. They eventually discovered what had guided them through the painful period of the pandemic. One of my clients managed to triple in size during COVID-19, while another renegotiated their contracts with clients and secured years of business. They chose to thrive and succeeded in achieving it.

Life is unpredictable, the good and the bad.

It is our choice if we choose to fight it, escape it, paste a smile on it despite the pain, or conquer it.

Authoring your life is a choice to love the life you have.

Authoring your story reveals the unique talent you have to give to this world.

It is a choice not to be someone else.

It is a choice not to envy others.

It is a choice to overcome the impostor syndrome we may feel sometimes.

It is a choice to listen to the voices of gratitude shared with you and build on them.

It is a choice to seek the good news first.

It is a choice not to blame other parties (even if you are right to do so) but to instead muster your power and transform your life into a story full of color and lessons.

It is a choice to refuse to be a victim in your own story and instead to rewrite this role to become the hero.

*Your story can be one you are proud to live and share,*

*a story that will make a difference in people's lives,*

*and a story of hope*

*only YOU can author.*

# With Gratitude

The first expression of gratitude is to Ben Salzman. He knew about this book before I did.

Any creative work is a work in progress influenced by so many people and experiences. In my professional and personal work, I had the privilege of working with employees, leaders, executives, and friends and family members who have influenced my thinking and life perspective and contributed in different ways to creating this story. You are too many to list, but gratitude is what I owe you all for opening your hearts and minds. Thank you for sharing your experiences with me.

Special thanks to Arestia Rosenberg for transforming my chaotic manuscript into the book you are reading now. I truly appreciate your passion and professionalism during the editing process. Thank you also to Brit McGinnis for your excellent line editing.

Thank you to my publisher, Greenleaf Book Group, and specifically Haj Chenzira-Pinnock, Adrianna Hernandez, Sally Garland, Pam Nordberg, Lauren Smith, Madelyn Myers, and Kristine Peyre-Ferry.

Thank you, God. To my dear family, who are the living chapters of my life's story: Dalya, Cheli, Liad, Netanel, Ronya, Jack, Benny, Boaz, Yoshi, Naveh—thank you for allowing me to write my life's story. To my dearest partner in life, my wife Drora, thank you for the journey. It is an experience.

# Notes

## Chapter 1

1. Daniel Kahneman and Amos Tversky, "Prospect Theory: An Analysis of Decision under Risk," *Econometrica* 47, no. 2 (March 1979): 263–292, https://doi.org/10.2307/1914185.

2. "Fight or Flight: How Employees Cope with Organizational Change," Arizona State University, October 24, 2007, https://news .wpcarey.asu.edu/20071024-fight-or-flight-how-employees -cope-organizational-change; Michael Nixon, "Fight, Flight, and Freeze: Human Responses in a Business Strategy Environment" (Honors Thesis, Brigham Young University, April 2019), https://scholarsarchive.byu.edu/cgi/viewcontent.cgi?article=1294 &context=studentpub.

## Chapter 3

1. P. R. Clance and S. A. Imes, "The Imposter Phenomenon in High Achieving Women: Dynamics and Therapeutic Intervention," *Psychotherapy: Theory, Research & Practice* 15, no. 3 (1978): 241–247, https://doi.org/10.1037/h0086006.

## Chapter 4

1.  Dan Gilbert, "The Psychology of Your Future Self," TED.com, March 2014, https://www.ted.com/talks/dan_gilbert_the _psychology_of_your_future_self?hasSummary=true.

## Chapter 8

1.  Ken Manktelow, *The Life, Times and Work of Peter Wason, Pioneering Psychologist* (London: Routledge, 2020); Julia Simkus, "Confirmation Bias in Psychology: Definition & Examples," Simply Psychology, updated June 22, 2023, https://www.simplypsychology.org/ confirmation-bias.html.

2.  Yona Goodman, *Mahapechat Hakeshev* (Hebrew) (*The Listening Revolution*) (Israel, Dvir: 2021).

3.  Monica Van Such, Robert Lohr, Thomas Beckman, James M. Naessens, "Extent of Diagnostic Agreement among Medical Referrals," *Journal of Evaluation in Clinical Practice* 23, no. 4 (August 2017): 870–874, doi: 10.1111/jep.12747.

## Chapter 9

1.  "Rabbi Sacks on Finding Purpose" (video), RabbiSacks.org, March 2010, https://rabbisacks.org/videos/rabbi-sacks-on-finding -purpose-jinsider/.

## Chapter 10

1.  OU Relief Missions (website), accessed March 9, 2024, https:// oureliefmissions.org/.

2. Ben Dean, PhD, "Defining Courage," University of Pennsylvania: Authentic Happiness, accessed March 6, 2024, https://www .authentichappiness.sas.upenn.edu/newsletters/authentic happinesscoaching/courage.

3. R. I. Fitzhenry, ed., *The Harper Book of Quotations* (New York: Harper Perennial, 1993), 110.

## Chapter 11

1. Jon D. Elhai, Jason C. Levine, Robert D. Dvorak, and Brian J. Hall, "Fear of Missing Out, Need for Touch, Anxiety and Depression Are Related to Problematic Smartphone Use," *Computers in Human Behavior* 63 (2016): 509–516, https://psycnet.apa.org/doi/10.1016/ j.chb.2016.05.079.

## Chapter 16

1. "What Is DiSC? Deepen Your Understanding of Yourself and Others," DiSC Profile.com, accessed March 6, 2024, https://www .discprofile.com/what-is-disc#what.

## Chapter 19

1. Margaret Samu, "Impressionism: Art and Modernity," The Met, October 2004, https://www.metmuseum.org/toah/hd/imml/ hd_imml.htm.

## Chapter 20

1. Rabbi Jonathan Sacks, *To Heal a Fractured World: The Ethics of Responsibility* (New York: Penguin Random House/Schocken Books, 2005).

## Chapter 21

1. Steven Bartlett, "Simon Sinek: The Number One Reason Why You're Not Succeeding," May 22, 2022, in *The Diary of a CEO with Steven Bartlett*, podcast, MP3 audio, episode 145, https://podcasts.apple.com/gb/podcast/e145-simon-sinek-the-number-one-reason-why-youre-not/id1291423644?i=1000563225737.

## Chapter 22

1. "Jews, Japan, Boycotts and Bigotry," *Chicago Tribune*, April 28, 1987, https://www.chicagotribune.com/news/ct-xpm-1987-04-28-8702010709-story.html.

2. Michael Timms, "Blame Culture Is Toxic. Here's How to Stop It," *Harvard Business Review*, February 9, 2022, https://hbr.org/2022/02/blame-culture-is-toxic-heres-how-to-stop-it.

3. Neil Farber, "5 Ways Blaming Hurts Relationships . . . ," *Psychology Today*, March 16, 2013, https://www.psychologytoday.com/us/blog/the-blame-game/201303/5-ways-blaming-hurts-relationships.

4. Robert I. Sutton, "Blame Is Contagious, Except When People Have High Self-Worth," *Psychology Today*, March 27, 2010, https://www.psychologytoday.com/us/blog/work-matters/201003/blame-is-contagious-except-when-people-have-high-self-worth.

## Chapter 25

1. Jenny Santi, "The Secret to Happiness Is Helping Others," Time.com, 2017, https://time.com/collection/guide-to-happiness/4070299/secret-to-happiness/.

2. Liudmila Titova and Kennon M. Sheldon, "Happiness Comes from Trying to Make Others Feel Good, Rather Than Oneself," *The Journal of Positive Psychology* 17, no. 3 (March 8, 2021): 341–355, doi: 10.1080/17439760.2021.1897867.

3. Molly McDonough, "What We Get When We Give," *Harvard Medicine*, October 2023, https://magazine.hms.harvard.edu/articles/what-we-get-when-we-give.

## Chapter 27

1. Te-Ping Chen, "Better Pay and Career Paths Drive U.S. Workers' Decisions to Quit," *The Wall Street Journal*, March 9, 2022, https://www.wsj.com/articles/why-workers-are-quitting-their-jobs-higher-paychecks-promotions-great-resignation-11646838499.

2. Leigh Branham, *The 7 Hidden Reasons Employees Leave: How to Recognize the Subtle Signs and Act Before It's Too Late* (New York: AMACOM, 2012).

3. Emi Nietfeld, "There's a Good Chance You'll Regret Quitting Your Job," *The Atlantic,* March 11, 2023, https://www.theatlantic.com/ideas/archive/2023/03/great-resignation-quit-job-regret/673346/.

## Chapter 29

1. "People-Pleasing," *Psychology Today*, accessed May 24, 2021, https://www.psychologytoday.com/us/basics/people-pleasing.

## Chapter 30

1. David W. Galenson, *Old Masters and Young Geniuses: The Two Life Cycles of Artistic Creativity* (Princeton, NJ: Princeton University Press, 2006).

## Chapter 31

1. Viktor E. Frankl, *Man's Search for Meaning* (Boston: Beacon Press, 1946).

# Index

## A

# W

Wason, Peter Cathcart, 68
Whac-A-Mole metaphor, 53
"What We Get When We Give"
 article, 193
Williamson, Marianne, 64
Williams, Vanessa, 41
wisdom storytellers, 230–32
word choices, 131–37
 categories of, 133–35
  celebratory and exciting, 135
  compassionate and
   forgiving, 134
  demanding and
   uncompromising, 134
  detail-oriented, 134
  emotional, 134
  inspirationally
   motivational, 134
  pain-focused, 135
  respect-for-journey, 134
  results-oriented, 133

changing, 136–37
factors that influence, 135–36
overview, 131–32
shutdown terminology, 132
work story, 203–8
 committment to mission and
  goals, 204–5
 employee-initiated
  movements, 203–4
 museum visitor analogy, 205–6
 values and purpose in
  workplace, 205–8
"world against me" attitude, 52
Wright, Frank Lloyd, 227

# Z

Zuckerberg, Mark, 41

# About the Author

One of the world's leading authorities on customer experience, transformation, and change, and founder of transformation firm Strativity Group, Lior Arussy has helped some of the world's leading brands write the next chapter in their story through the transformative process. Arussy's clients include Mercedes-Benz, Delta Airlines, Royal Caribbean Cruises, BMW, Cadillac, Novo Nordisk, MasterCard, The Met, Thomson Reuters, HSBC, E.ON, FedEx, SAP, and Johnson & Johnson, among others.

Recipient of several awards, Arussy is the author of seven books, including *Next Is Now: 5 Steps for Embracing Change—Building a Business That Thrives into the Future* (May 2018, Simon & Schuster), *Exceptionalize It!* (2015), and *Customer Experience Strategy: The Complete Guide from Innovation to Execution* (2010). Arussy has written over four hundred articles for publications around the world, including the *Harvard Business Review*, and has been interviewed by MSNBC, CNBC, Bloomberg TV, the *Wall Street Journal*, *Fast Company*, *CRM*, *Smart CEO*, and *Inc.* magazine.